If you're heading out to sea, stash this book in your duffel bag before you go. You'll need something to entertain yourself and the crew on a long saltwater voyage.

Seventeen haiku (one for each syllable of a haiku), twenty-four poems, and two songs make up this collection of eclectic writings. Destination: the uncharted oceans of the imagination.

The subjects include rabbit holes, flying metal boxes, churches, trees, the Higgs Boson particle, squirrels, underwear, and sea odysseys. My photography and drawings accompany each poem.

Take advantage of the wind and tide. Sail on!

Haiku, Schmaiku, and Headin' Out to Sea
by David Robert Bayard

Published in-house April Fools' Day, 2019

Copyright by Skyboy Press | Kansas City, Missouri

International Standard Book Number (ISBN) 978-0-9967380-8-8

Cover art by David Bayard
Front cover: Ink on Paper
Back cover: Digital photography of two spiderwebs being woven in the morning sun
All photographs and drawings by David Bayard

Thanks to Deborah Shouse and Emily Iorg-Walters for their help
in preparing this manuscript to greet the world,
and to Amory Bottorff for musical notation on "Sea Shanty" and "Sailor".

Also by David Bayard from Skyboy Press:

"Sky Stories: The Sky and Nature Calendar" published annually since 2015.
"Gathering the Self: Poems of the Heart" © 2018
All publications available at www.skyboyphotos.com/Books

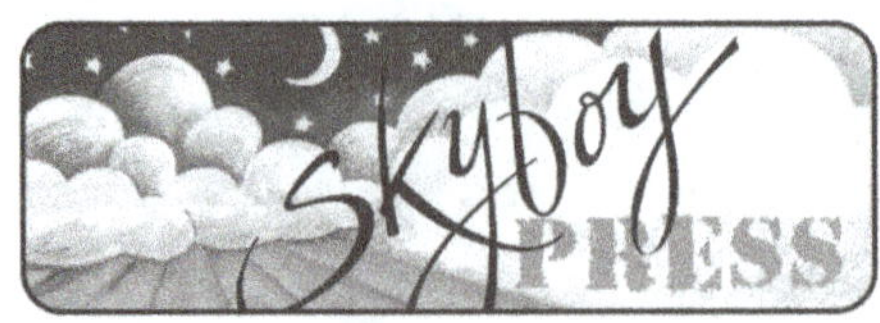

Haiku, Schmaiku
and Headin' Out to Sea

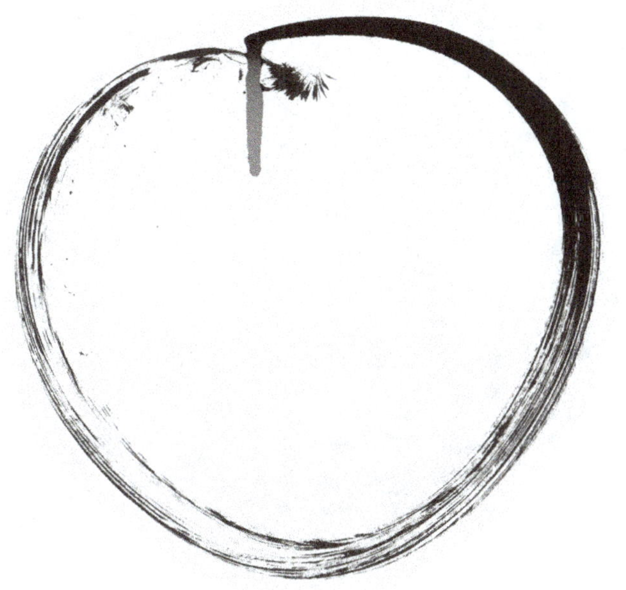

Poetry as Looking Glass
Poetry as Mirror

Table of Contents

Three ~ Mirror   103

Introduction

You can do this too. Try it. Grab a writing utensil and a purchased journal, or a notebook, or an old envelope, or a napkin from the coffee shop. Write what you feel. Write what you have. Write down who you are.

Do it once or make a habit. If you do it once, you may be drawn into the habit. Not just when you feel like it, but—the most helpful—when you don't. I suggest journal writing, keeping a personal record of your scribbles on some regular basis. Writing it all down is a great way to preserve, sort out, and examine your thoughts and feelings from a different perspective. It allows, on a playing field level, wrestling with the puzzles and the problems that bedevil.

Don't worry about making it public. Do it whether or not you ever intend to share. Sharing with yourself is the whole point.

These poems of mine may look finished now, but you should have seen them when first written, full of mud, drivel, and flatulence! They came spewing out bloody and raw and had to be worked and cleaned, healed of their rawness and mess before they could be called finished, with all the extraneous placenta digested.

So don't give a thought to how your writing looks. Put it in the refrigerator if you need to and take it out again next week. Look at it again. Once it's thawed, taste it, touch it, smell it. Read yourself.

Just take the leap. Write.

The Cover Page

After fifteen tries, the calligraphy was perfect.
I stood it up proudly on the easel stand.
Big mistake. I came back in the morning to find the ink had run.
Why didn't I lay it flat? What's wrong with me? It's ruined!
Because you didn't. Nothing. No, it isn't.
I realized the only thing affected was my fragile ego. The perfect ink-on-paper Zen circle knew exactly what it was doing.
So I honored the mistake with the color of blood. Like a wound. A boo-boo, an accident, an opening, a portal, a possibility.
Flaws in oysters make pearls. Goofs in DNA strands make new types of creatures. Errors in any endeavor when correctly perceived can lead to astounding and unforeseen creative breakthroughs.
So go on, flubs, blunders, gaffes, faux pas, keep coming. I welcome you. It means I'm human. Like everyone.

The Poems

They came as lost and lonely children begging for some porridge, for nourishment, for life, to fix their broken parts by loving them exactly as they are.

Or: they came already formed and trusted I could unpack them, polish off the dust and dirt of travel, then put them on the high display shelf without breaking them.

Or: they came as prompts, from myself or from others, as a spur to
the flow of creative juices of black ink.

Or: they began with an idea but then proceeded to fly off on a tangent
of their own, swaying and swooping in random trajectories with no
consideration for what I had originally planned.

Haiku was a fun thing that I thought to try,
Seventeen in number, each with seventeen syllables,
Making that many ways to boil down a moment,
Expunging the extraneous to reveal
The simple essence at its heart.
And in this my first rough attempt, I plainly see
Why the sages call it art.

Two of the poems, "Sea Shanty" and "Sailor", came with music and
should rightly be called songs.

Three poems are elegies to those I love who have moved
Beyond the gate, and for whose presence, touch and voice
I long but for which I guess I'll have to wait:
My good friends Jon and Raymond of so many years,
And fellow poet Mary, who has oft moved me to tears

Then we have a number of other poems that have nothing particular
in common other than their poem-ness. I have corralled them all, hai-
ku, schmaiku and sea songs, into three areas where they shall remain
unless they succeed in digging their way under the fencing:

~ Looking Glass ~

First there is seeing the world with new eyes for subtle things: The
way that birdsong rings, the scattered diamonds of the stars, beheld
alike by brides and beggars, bards and kings; a river running deep
and strong past a shore that moves the other way. For we need not so
much to change the world as to see it yet anew every day.

~ Double Lens ~

Second is relationship, that complicated mathematics that obeys
chaos theory; where small things can enlarge to more than their total
sum; where every action makes an opposite unequal, unpredictable,
unparalleled in grace; and where two beings, separate, as they grow
toward one another, create something new, a third divinity that re-
sembles neither solitary face.

~ Mirror ~

Third is the act of reflection as consciousness watches itself watching
itself: the use of writing, journaling, and poetry to gaze into the mir-
ror, see ourselves as others see us, and find the universal truths of the
mystic that are inherent in every spirit.

Enough talk about the writing. Go read 'em.
I hope with all my heart they tickle yours.

One

Looking Glass

Begin

Page just sits there blank.
Pen is staring. What to do?
Open fear and write.

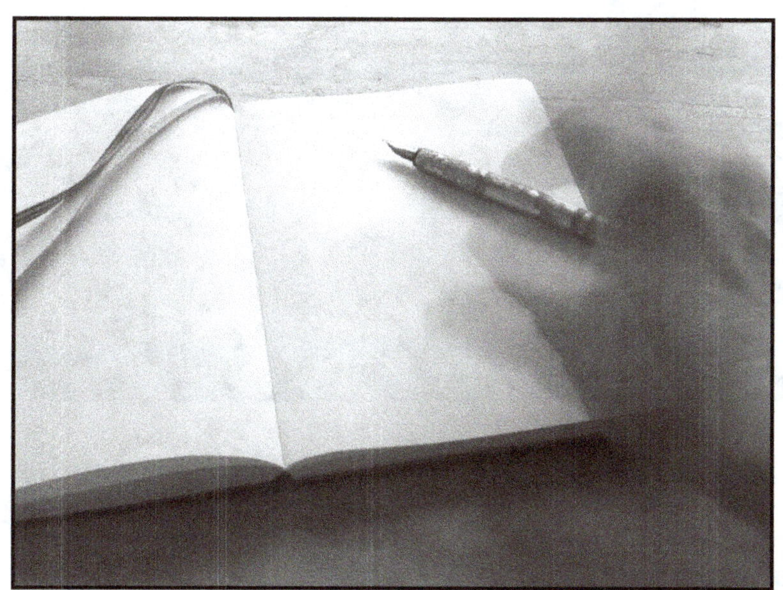

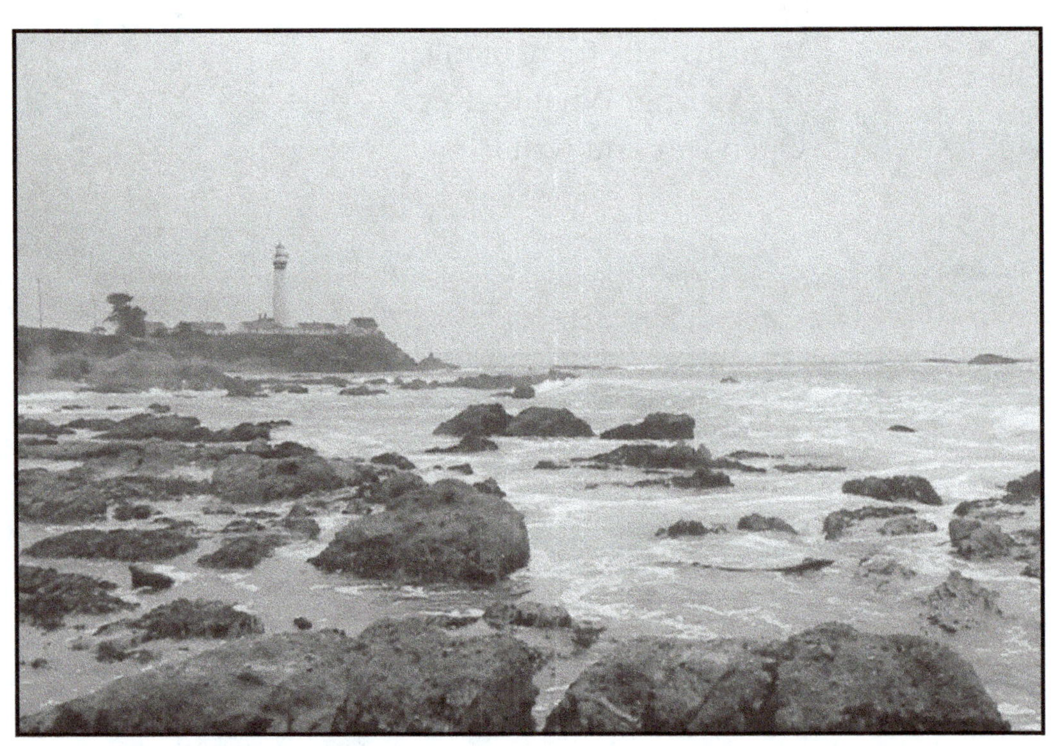

Sailor

Verse 1

Oh, the sea may call you to sail her
Though she's deep, stormy, and wide
Embark on a personal odyssey
On the uncharted ocean inside
Let your pain fill the sails, your trust turn the wheel
And honesty be your guide
Bring flint for the match and oil for the lamp
For to see the true self by your side.

Verse 2

Perhaps it's a wound or a sorrow
You find you can no longer hide
Or an endless season of winter
Whose presence will not be denied
Whatever the reason, if this is your season
Then cast off and flow with the tide
Let the sea carry you into the eye
Of the storms that are raging inside

Chorus 1

If you go out to sea but you hang by the shoals
And you stand in the lee and give up on your goals,
Your dreams will then wither and die
The ones where you dreamed you could fly
And to the dark
you'll remain irretrievably tied.

So be brave like Odysseus, move in deep water
Recall that you are the sea's sons and her daughters
You are the same, can't you tell,
In every movement and swell?
You are the waves
And she is the reason for tides.

  Verse 3

Your friends will ask why you wander
Where so many others have died
It will seem like a bad decision
But it's not something someone decides
So they'll think that you're leaving and they'll begin grieving,
Believing it's just suicide
Forgive them for not knowing what you must do
It's all because they never tried.

  Verse 4

Abandon the lands that you've known
The signposts on which you've relied
Scuttle the cargo of falsehoods
Given by those who implied
That the course that was set for you was what was best for you
Now you can see they lied.
So stitch the dark clouds in a big canvas shroud
And heave them all over the side

  Chorus 2

If you're sore tempted by seductive sirens
Singing their songs while you're in the environs

Then fasten yourself to the mast
And have the crew tie you down fast
Until you have passed,
Remain as you are safely tied.

When the chart says beware, that there be monsters there
You may find monsters inside everywhere.
They're only the shadows you cast
Be glad that you've found them at last.
Befriend your dark half
And keep him right there at your side

Verse 5

Gather support where you find it
Recognize those on your side
There's no glory in sailing alone
There's no shame in engaging a guide
For it's a riddle you're wrapped in, and though you're the cap-
tain
You still need a crew by your side.
Seek out the souls who have sailed the seas
Use the wisdom that they can provide.

Chorus 3

Learn to relax and to bend like a willow
Discover your tenderness, make it your pillow
Let softness of heart be your shield
Heart is strongest when willing to yield
As the hero of Troy
When despairing just broke down and cried

Be brave like Ulysses, leave fear in your wake
Be like the mast which will bend but not break
Look to the sky and observe
How the birds rest their wings in the curve
Of the wind
Then follow the currents they ride.

   Verse 7 (End)

If the sea should call you to sail her
Know she's deep, stormy, and wide
Embark on your personal odyssey
On the uncharted ocean inside
Let your pain fill the sail, your trust hold the wheel
And honesty be your guide
Bring flint for the match and oil for the lamp
   For to see the true self
   For to love the true self
   For to be the true self by your side.

Sailor

Transcription by Amory Bottorff

Verse

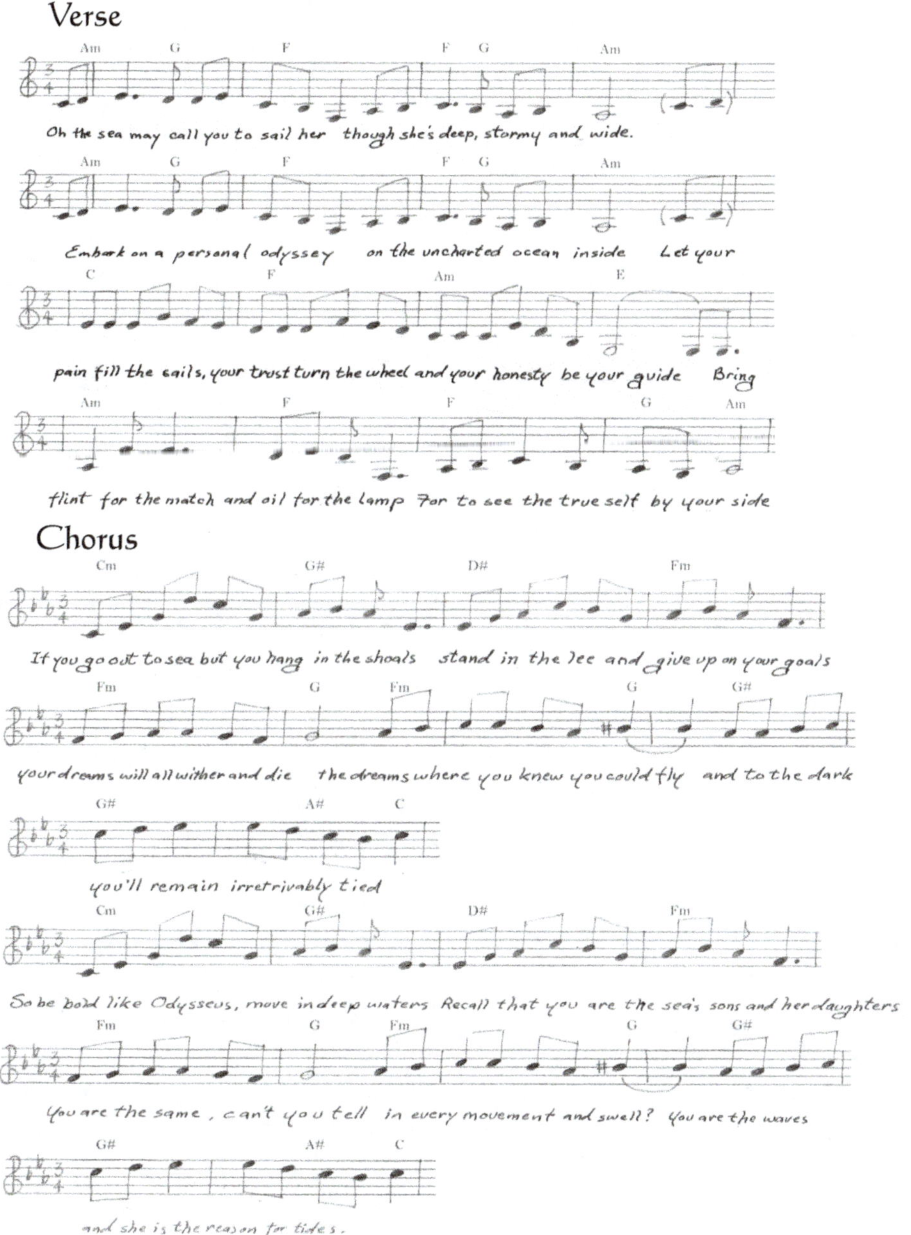

Chorus

Rose

My nose becomes drunk
In the loosened folds of the
Rose's velvet gown

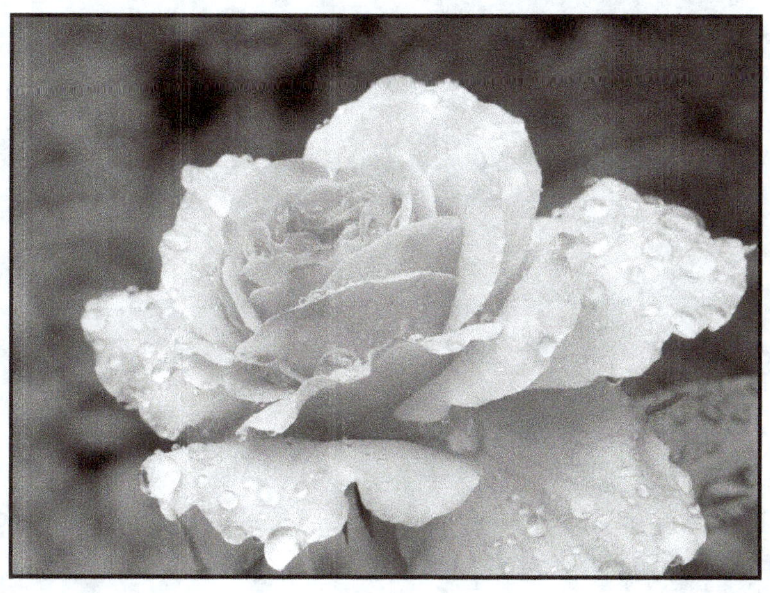

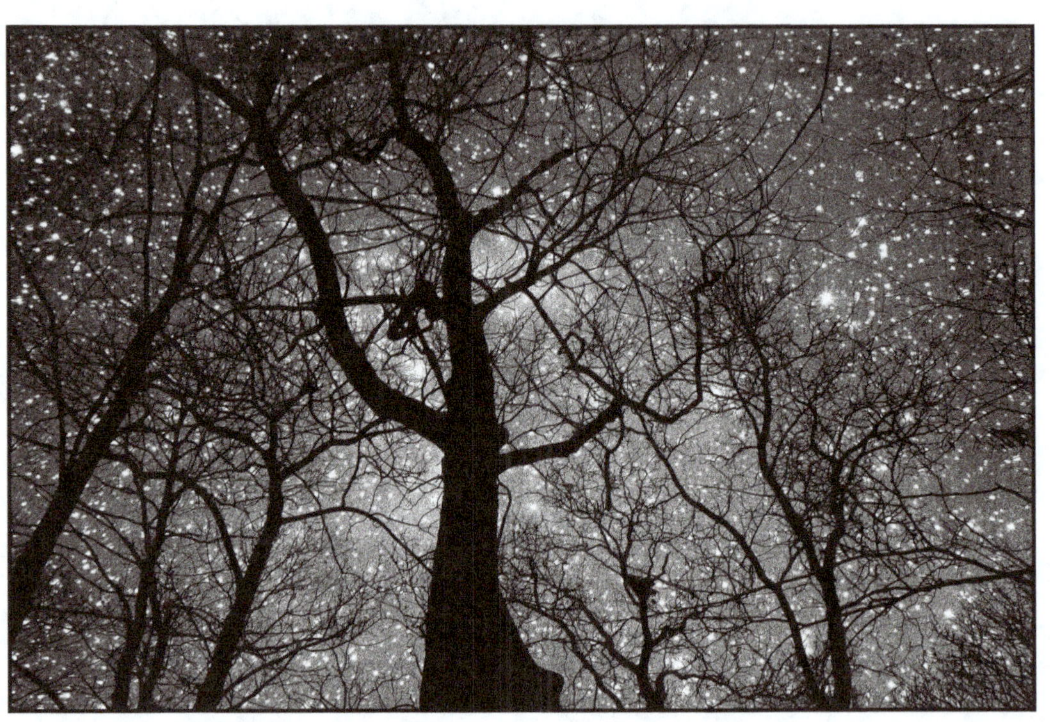

A Wild Night

A chill wind slips by razor-sharp, nicks my cheeks in passing.
  The stars wheel in orbits 'round the barren limbs of trees.

I am smitten with a yearning for adventure as it
  strops one side then another of some secret inner blade.

I love the leaves leaping from their limbs to
  climb upon the wind, dragging stars behind them as they
    scrape across the greying whale skin of sky!

I see my own two limbs rise upward, the fingers of my hands
  like lotus blossoms open, reaching out to
    fling wide the waiting gate of heaven.

The sweet and sour taste of all eternity is enfolded in the now,
  this sacred moment in the infinite unrolling in my life.

I will no longer build my walls of castle, brick by weighty brick,
  nor clutch the torment of my schedules or my needless reasons.
    I release them, for they've outlived their seasons.

Plumbing deep the heart's true measure here within
  the wilderness is heaven early dropped to earth.

Wanderlust for vast uncharted territories fills my soul with wildness.
  This shall be my prime and lusty purpose evermore.

Long-silent words cry out beneath the hollow dome of pewter
  darkness and echo through the trees: relax your fist,
    release your hold on fate.

Let it work its will within your body. Let it lift you to the wind.

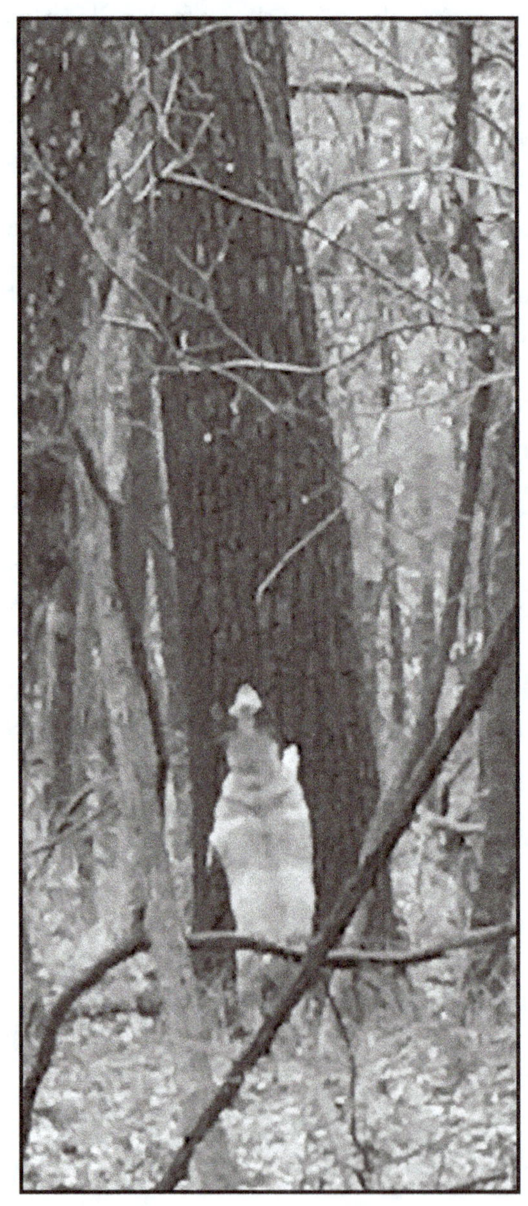

The Chase

"I spies 'im!" she cries, as she races out
  across the forest floor.
Like lightning o'er the leaves she dashes
  to the broad base of the tree.
By then the clever creature is on the other side,
  invisible to her, bolting up and out of sight.
She gazes round the earth below
  bewildered,
Looks up and down but cannot see her quarry,
  nary found.
She circles round the tree in spinning eager arcs
  as her wily foe circumnavigates behind,
   ever hidden as the far side of the moon.
  Then he flings his body upward, disappears.
Moments later treetops rustle with his flight, though
  she's not sleuth enough to spot him.
Soon five trees away, he is flying branch to branch,
His bright grey tail flitting like a majorette's advance.
She leaps! She leaps again upon the tree's broad bole!
In vain, for she has been outsquirrelled.
  Though she's lost 'im,
   desperate she dashes to every falling twig,
  each flicking leaf in wind's embrace, any likely place
   where the wily flying thing could be surprised again.

  But he is nowhere in her world.
Far away I spy him, flag unfurled, taunting
  my good dog in whom joy yet reigns supreme,
   and who undaunted noses through the wood toward
  the next encounter in this e'er delightful game!

Light

Sudden glint of sun
Rappels down the spiderweb,
Zip-lines back and forth

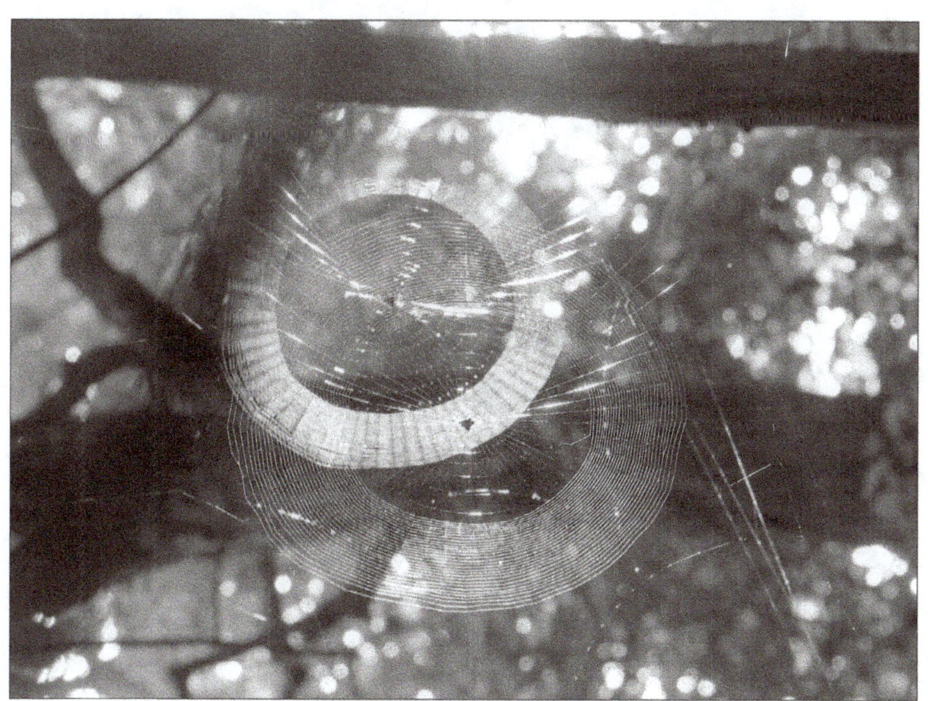

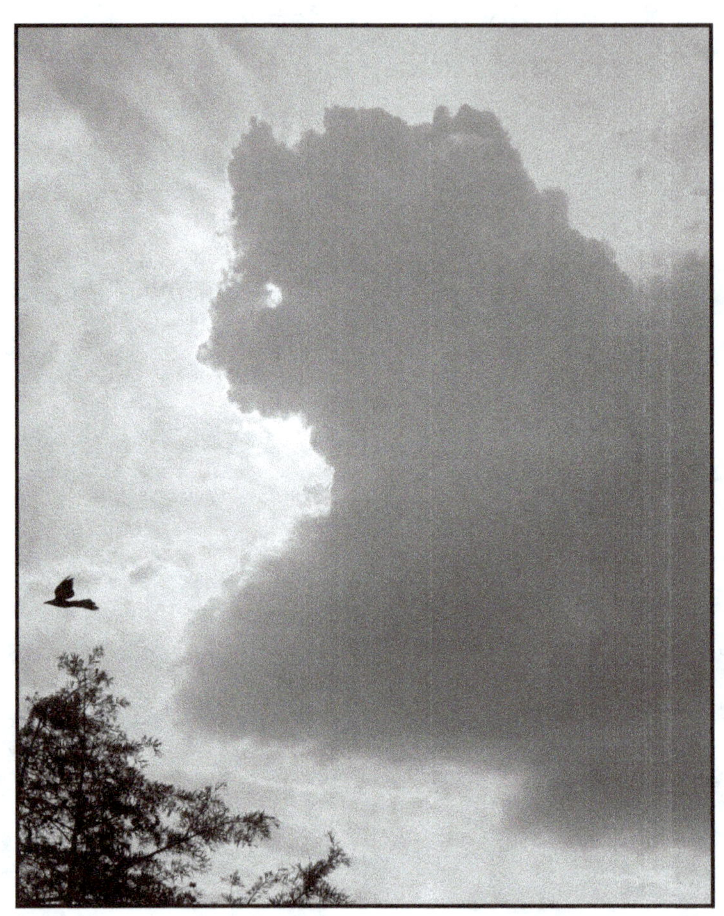

The Bird Is a Bible

The bird is a bible of movement in air
We read her but partly and then she's not there
Her light holy grace has flown on who knows where
Pray thee not plan
But leap as you can
And follow her up if you dare!

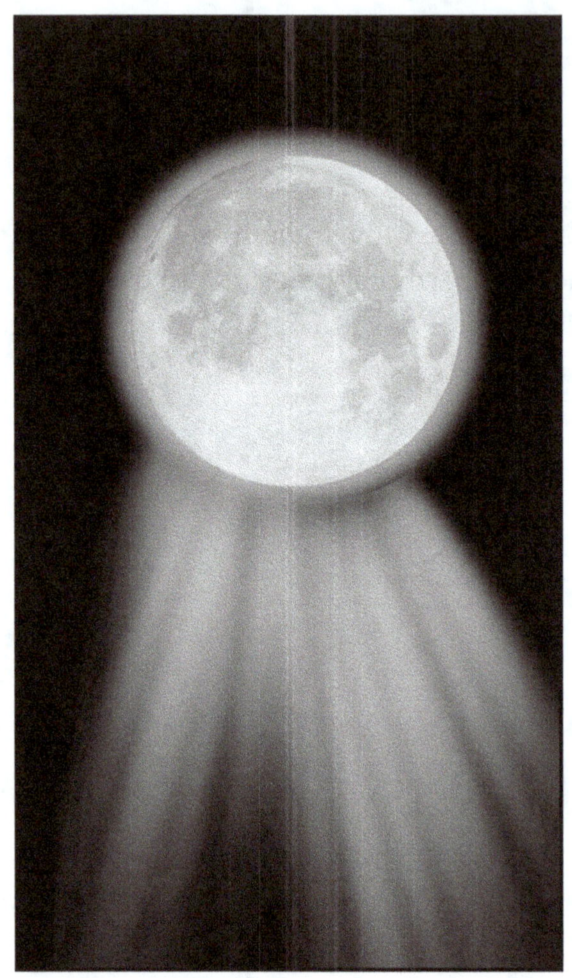

Luna

The shape of her body
  fills the night without
  time or language

She beams to earth a woman
  then displays her myriad of forms
  softened like the snow

Sometimes she is a man, sometimes
  a fish diving deep below
  the surface of the sea

Then she is a small boy sleepless
  near an open window, wondering,
  waiting for something to begin

Or a singer returning from a gig
  alone, jousting with the memory
  of his performance

Watch as she alights to paint
  her silver light upon any
  thought or object

Early dawn a shopkeeper is
    sweeping her off the front stoop
    but she playfully leaps back up

A seamstress stitching her into fine
    crinoline of wedding dress
    for some future unfolding

A trucker on the road picks up her signaling
    Morse code from behind the trees
    perhaps a frantic message to be careful

Now she comes spilling through my open window
    painting toes and fingers one by one
    as well the ruffled hillocks of bedsheet

She sits upon the chair across the room,
    leans in close and whispers quiet stories
    of encounters with her mother the world

That's her job, I suppose, to glide across night
    bringing all creatures closer in the dark,
    less lonely for having been kissed.

Pond

Frog, then splash! ~ no frog.
Pond jumps onto my arm ~
Basho visits me!

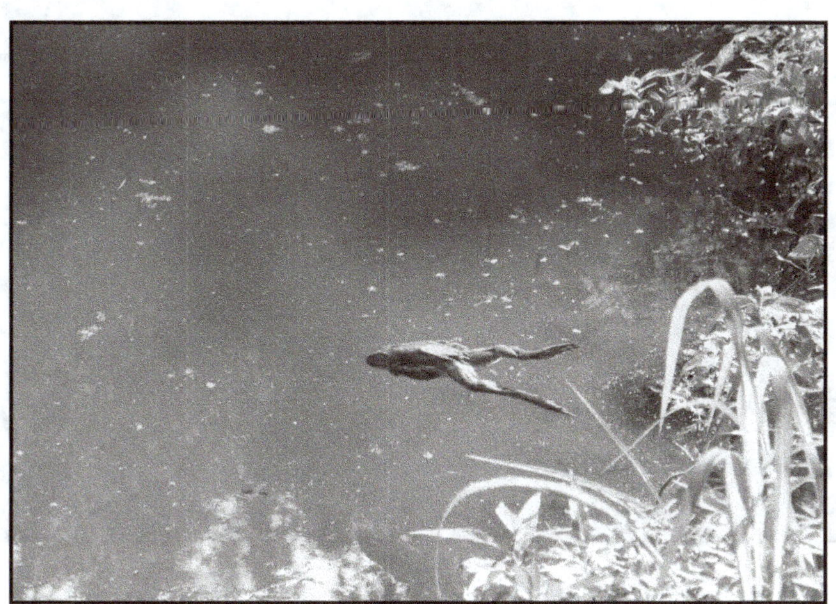

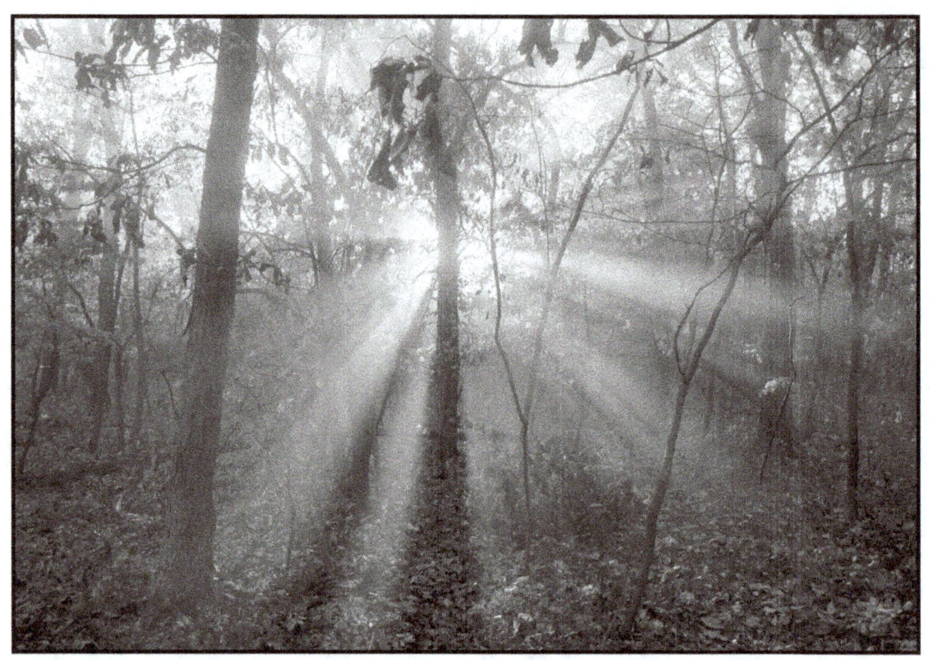

The Trees

The trees they are my champions.
    They raise their arms to take me in.
They see my cloud of doing,
    cloud of worry, and they wisely speak out
David, shed your skin.
Come into being, world of grace, and raise your arms to
        heaven.
    There is no other place to be than now and here.
You knew but have forgotten,
    and have anxiously been holding.
Now you know what it means to do or not to do.
    There is no person other than the one
        you are unfolding.
Slip beneath the fog to
    stand upon the ground of your own being,
    which has been waiting patiently and true.
If you turn your head upside-down you'll see the ground
    is also standing upon you.

There is no other world, they whisper.
You are the only you, and
        nothing in your being has to do,
nothing has to make or think or ponder or review.
Simply root yourself in wonder and be dazzled, as we do,
    and live each moment here anew.

    They stand in sweet array around me,
my body gently touching on their own.
    Underground we speak through funguses and smuts,
the little mini-mushrooms of the elves.
As a forest we may moan and turn
    and twist and bend within the wind
but it is not a doing,
    it is done.
We are not other than we are.
    We are finally tree enough
        and eternally are nothing but ourselves.

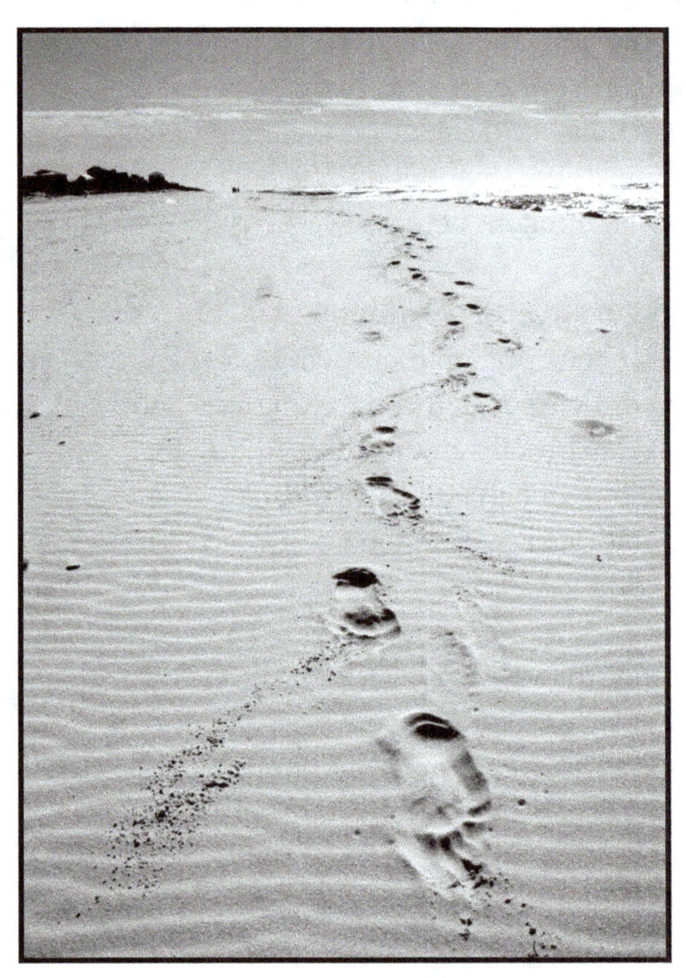

Be Ye The Sand

Be ye the sand on the beach without thinking, without figuring out. Just tumble along with the jumble of particles, a small participle in that magnificent sentence as it rolls across the limitless tongue of the shore.

Be ye the black limbs of trees waving leafless in the wind, without asking questions, without needing answers. Just be the limbs. Be the trees.

Be ye the last leaf pulled to the sky, punching into the wildness, knocking back down to the sand and into the air in a mad unknowing of where you are heading or why. Simply obey what you are.

Be ye the winds from the far four corners of the wide rim of the earth. Be ye the cardinal points of the mystery. For the sand, the leaves, the sea, and the stars have a wisdom that guides your body as it flies to and fro in the wind.

Reason has such a short season, there is no time for this questioning. But time and time and time for the rest lives on in the greatest abundance.

Just be yourself as you are when you're true to your God. Caress the face of your God as if the soft face of a child, however your God rolled you up.

Be ye bound to your singular self as you embody the greater soul, that soul that's as big as the sea.

Leaf

Leaf wheeling through space
A galaxy free, tethered
To spider's lost strand

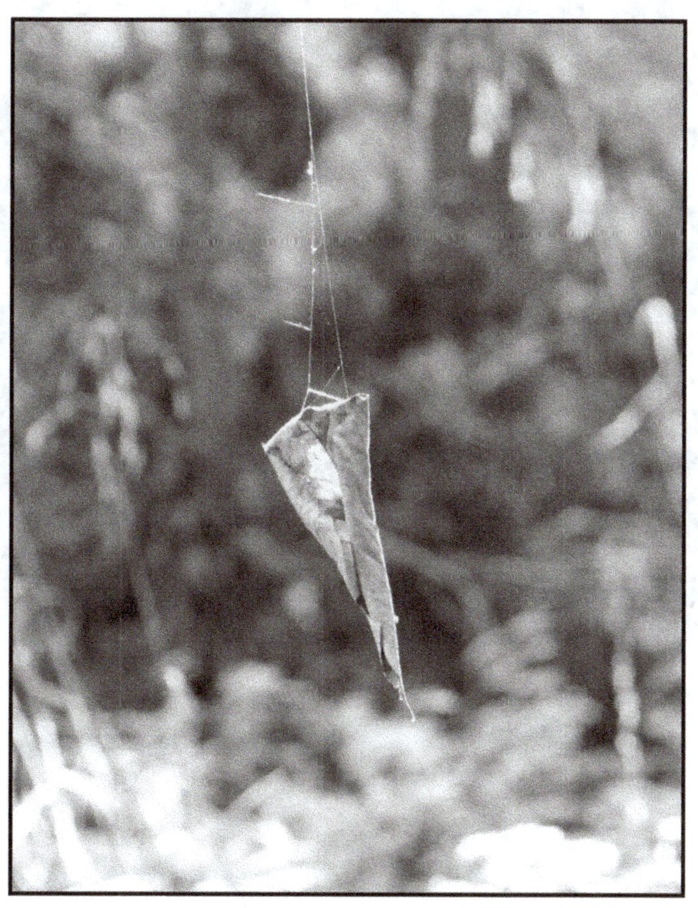

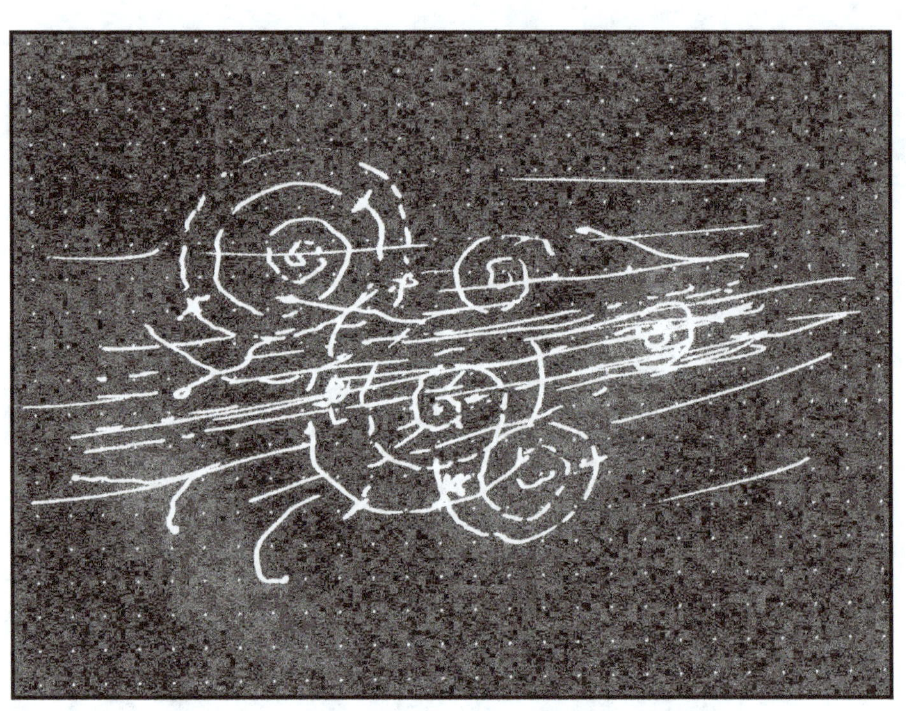

Higgs Boson

At its heart it's all a two-step dance
One-two, one-two, cha cha cha,
Sine wave up and sine wave down,
Both the same, opposing,
A simple moving circle.

No wonder the Higgs boson particle is
Called after God, for it gives mass to all other
Particles,
That mad soup of sea-foam in which we swim,
Which otherwise would move without resistance,
As hearts, when free of weight, will
Enlarge to ridiculous proportions and
Eventually lose the beat.

And from their mass comes friction,
Without which there would be no heat of struggle
In the gathering of a self. Muscles lose
All tone if not worked nor do they strengthen
Without effort, thus spirit
Could not sharpen unless honed against
The coarse rough stone of matter.

That's the simple physics of it, a particle
That calls the dance within this graceful elegance
So infinite in mystery,
That when seen and grasped with self-awareness
Can say simply of itself,

It Is What It Is.

Imbued within its complex structure is the
Selfsame thing which we name consciousness,
The science of our life, a budding tree of shy
Self-knowledge that can
Speak in tongues and sing aloud,

I Am That I Am.

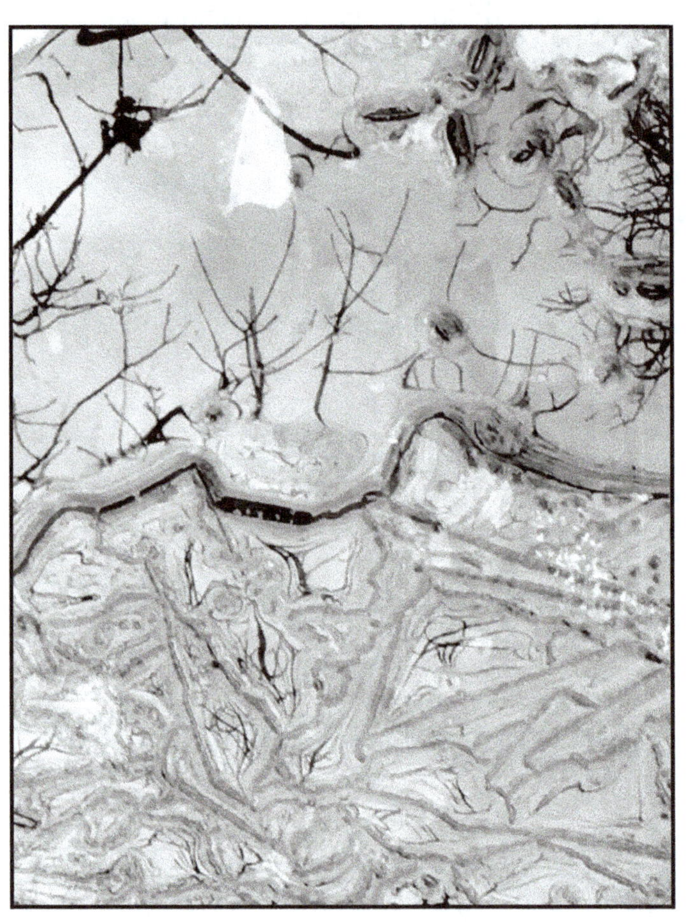

Blue Window

In my fish pond
  are two blues,
a milky blue of sky
  overlaid on deep cobalt
of water. Through a window
  in the leaf canopy reflected
by the water is a
  framed lithograph of heaven.
The far realm of air in this way
  introduces herself to that
other realm of the fluid,
  her twin sister Water.

Water and Air move in rhythm,
  bouncing off one another
in a kind of pas de deux.
  We could imagine it was we who,
taking their two hands in ours,
  would make the introduction.
"Water, meet tall sky, if you please,"
  and "Air, do say hello to the realm
of the seas," as if we were master of
  everyone else's ceremonies.

But they would not need us
   in order to meet one another
or their mother the Earth.
   Whether we choose as a people or
township, a tribe or a species,
   to stay here among them,
to meet them as neighbors,
   they will keep meeting, Air giving
bubbles to water and water her
   clouds to the air, every day chatting,
each day introducing themselves
   by saying in all sacred ways,
"Hello, my Air" and "Hello to you,
   good friend Water," as they have done
for these thousands of
   thousands of thousands of years
     with
       and then also
         without you.

Sky

Weather rules day, our
Neighbors, the night. Sky is both
Ocean and window.

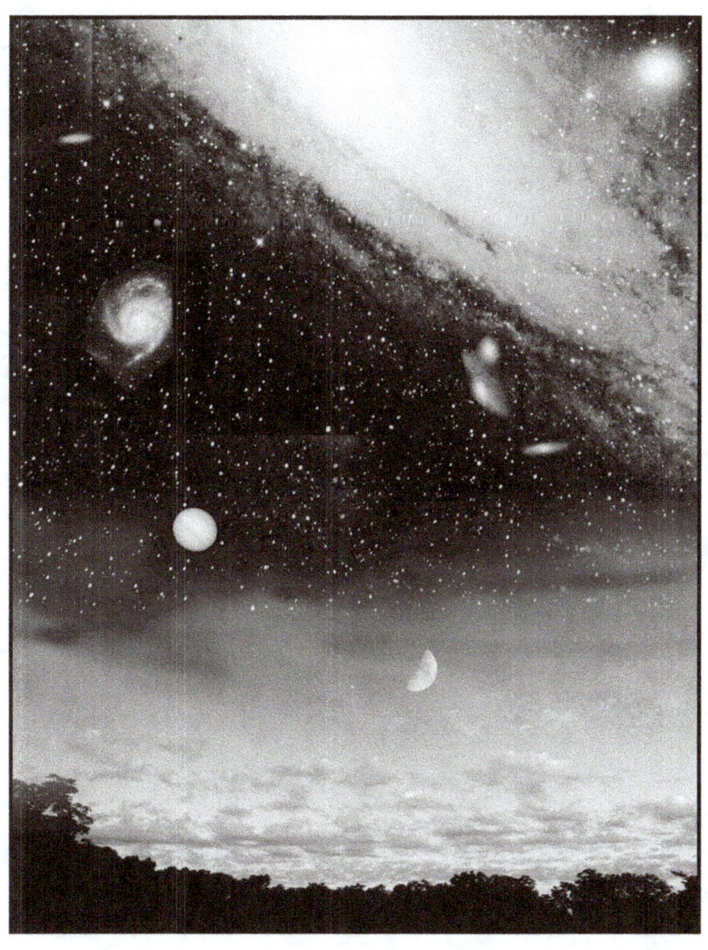

Two

Double Lens

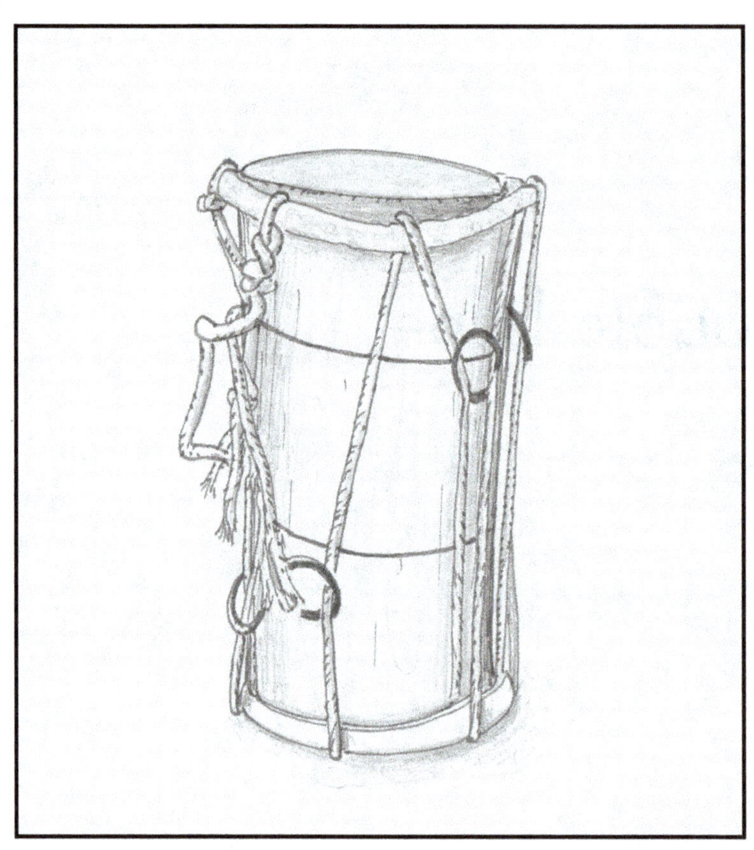

Beat the Drum of You

Before dusk arrives, before the night has fallen,
Beat your drum.
It will have as many rhythms as you've seen
Days that come and go,
Waves in their completion on the shore.

Beat the drum in all your ways,
Some so shy and dainty,
Some large and booming vast,
But all a part of you singing you.
In this letting go your inner beat is measured,
Marked in what you wear,
The masks you don and doff
And those that finally just wear off,
Exposing the true drummer at the center.

Let the beating of your heart compose
The song as it resolves around your ears.
Follow it as if you were a salmon in a stream,
Helpless, heeding heady summons of biology,
Enraptured with the being, no awareness
Of the doing.

Beat your drum.
        Beat it bravely in a rhythm
Solid as the clay that forms your bones,
Reverberating deeply in the hollow vessel that is you.

Be yourself, which is the hardest thing to do.

Magic

Morning sun through trees
Makes shoji lamp by doorway,
Then dissolves the trick

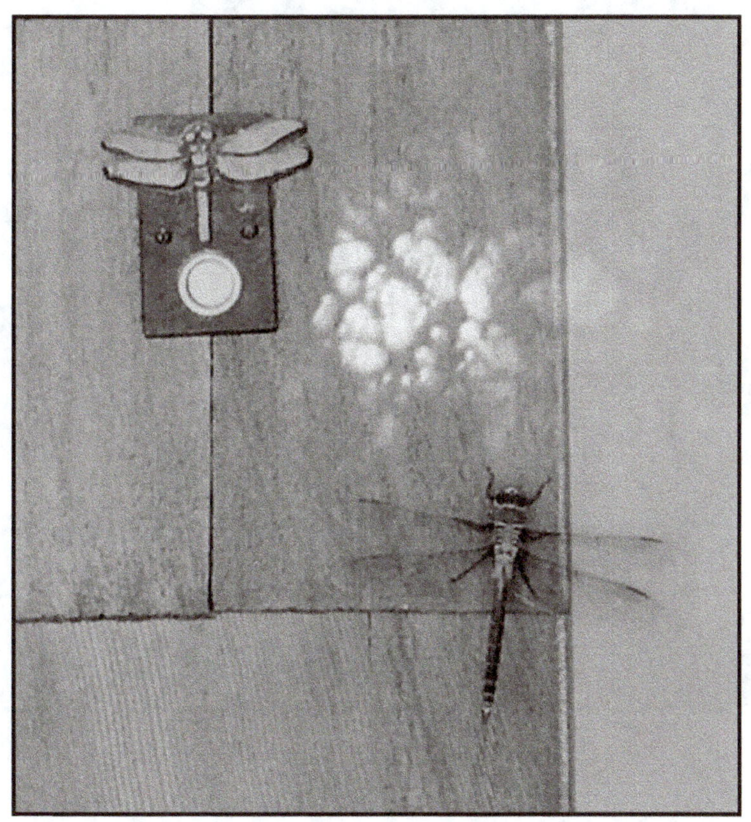

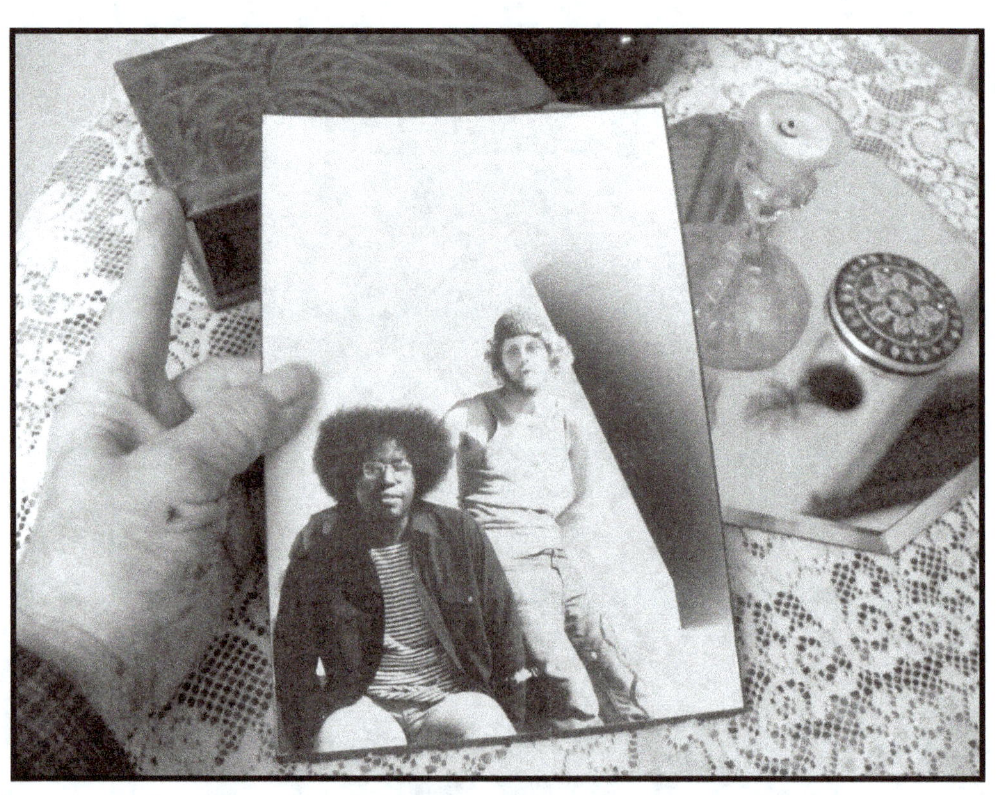

Crazy Love

For Jon Henry Conway, 1945-2018

His love made me big as everybody, in a way
this poem is not large enough to say.

I fluttered through his open door a wounded bird.
He saw my wings were crushed and took me in,
nurtured me in shoebox with some stuffing, bit of food,
where I could slowly heal my frame, establish some
relation to the name that I'd been given:
"David" means "Beloved."
His heart was like a creche where I was
born again into a life I owned.

In my room filled with Peter Max posters,
art deco, and a print of "The Dawn" by Maxfield Parrish,
that painting of two nymphs beside a pool,
one awakening the other to drink in the miracle
of a crystal morning under sky of bottle blue,
I was awakening as well to something new.
As Janis Joplin smashed her way out the turntable
to offer up another little piece of her heart,
Van Morrison sang of sailing
Into the Mystic, invoking Crazy Love while
we grew our own within the garden.

He stood guardian of my gate like

Colossus, fierce defender of my soul.
"Do not walk into his room as if you owned him!"
he roared to those who were used to
having their own way with me.
"Get out! Get the hell out of my house or
I will set your soul afire!"
He would suffer neither evil nor duplicity,
face up to men ten times his size until they
sniveled off like the cowards such men always are.
With a single nod he could let me know
when he sensed some evil in the room.

While I practiced with my wings,
he kept me safe from the users and abusers
and even well-meaning folks without a clue.
Mother, he protected me from you.
But let us not allow you in this poem.
This is his alone.
This is all I have to give him now,
the song of good Jon Henry.

I can still recall him humming tuneless songs
aimlessly in kitchen, as if he knew just how to be.
Such a simple act was
far beyond my complicated capability.
Standing, swaying, stirring black-eyed peas and
ham hocks, he was like a sprite or an elf within the wood
whose soul knew nothing but the good.

We each shared the parts of us the other needed most.
His Taurus Bull held my Water Bearer, shapeshifter

Aquarius, into a solid form that held,
and I'd like to think that I returned the gift, whereby
my art of water held that steady, sometimes stubborn
beast well balanced and afloat upon the sea as well.

He must have known that I would fly away
once I'd gained the strength to soar.
For I was like a child whose flag must be unfurled, must
someday leave their home to find a way into the world.
Did I ever know him? Or was it just
his image in my mirror, standing tall behind me
arms wrapped around as he lifted me to stand upon
the threshold he'd created.
As I leaped, he must have sensed that
he'd remain behind, not knowing if I'd ever
come a-runnin' back to him.
Van Morrison be damned, life is not as simple as a song.

I can see him in my mind, in my heart,
so like the beating heart of him,
having got and given love in full as it must be
when one has lived a life as large as he,
a life into which he folded me,
a life that knows that love is letting go.

His arms released and then mine opened.
He must have taught me well, for now that he is gone
I am learning letting go as well.

Solace

Fire escape is my
Only lonely companion
Save for the stairway

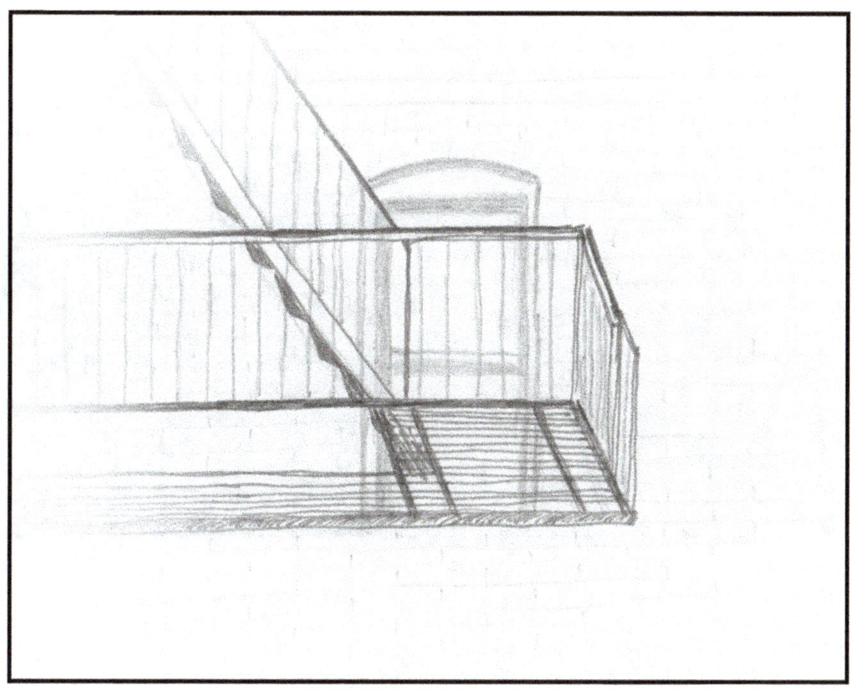

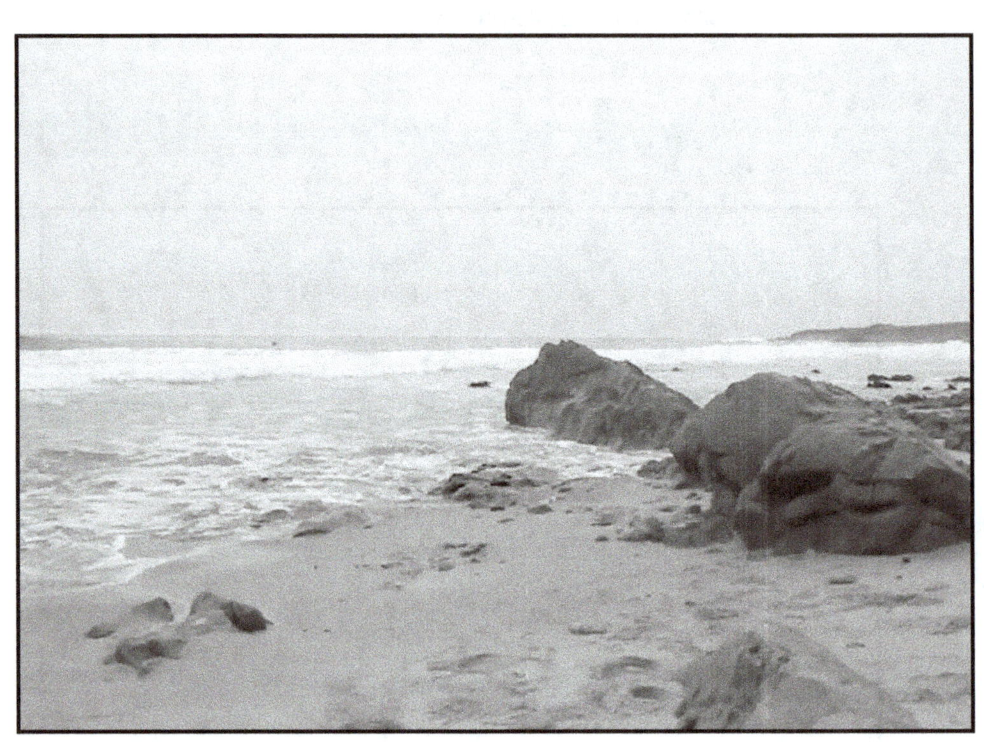

Odysseus Time

We floated by the rocks that we remembered
From Odysseus' time.
There by the Sirens' first sweet notes, tearing at our
Hearts with an innocence, a longing
So evermore and distantly recalled that
  we thought the songs were universal.
We paused, two bodies in the water with reflections.
Moments came, then receded, echoed back again.

Thus when a young maiden with violin did seat herself
upon the grassy outcrop and from her instrument
flower out a melody, I recognized the danger.
I called to you, "Watch out! Don't swim closer or we'll crash
upon the rocks!" I made you laugh.
She laughed, too. She must have studied the Greeks. We became
as gods and goddesses, there as water lapped at shore and
shore at water, our melody a joy like tinkling bells.

Did you want to remain longer or was it merely my
  lonely voice to myself calling?
As we bathed beneath the waterfall of sky,
  orange light settling toward the fading sun,
you turned to me, I to you, then both toward something wonderful,
  something other than ourselves
  but identical.

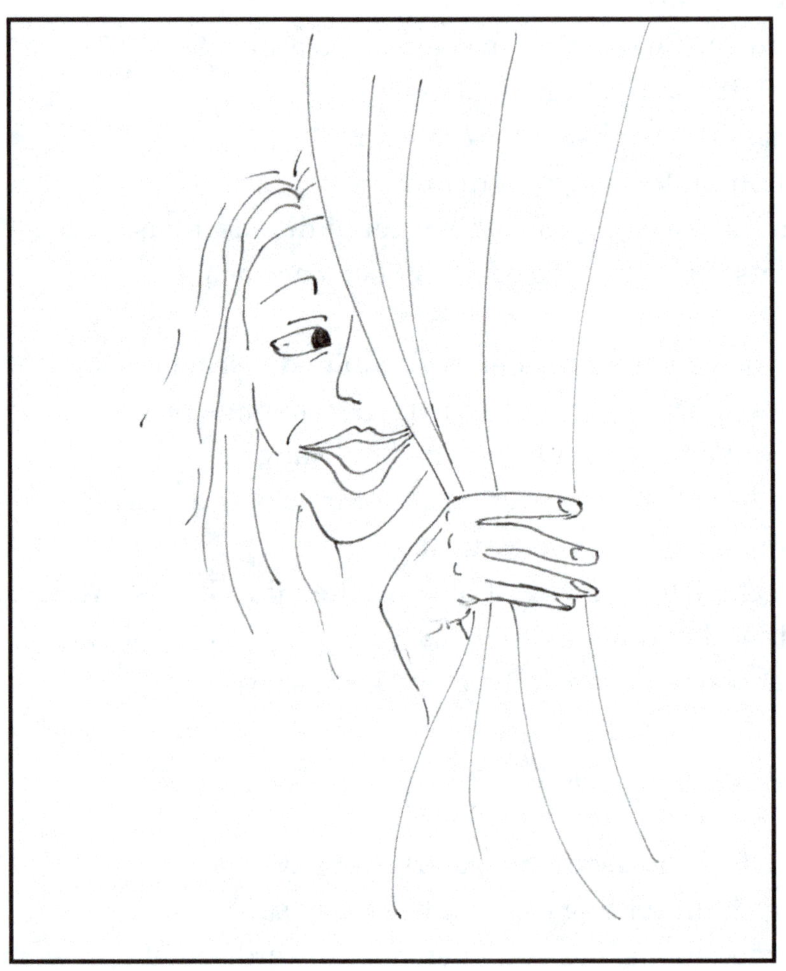

Underthings

I will hide it no more. You know,
  that unmentionable thing,
That lifelong secret part of us, that sweet
  sense of
              dizziness
    that somehow sits below the light of day
And keeps us all well hidden as we dither,
  we cover and we pray.
Sex
  is the word I dare not utter.
But I will hide no more.
My extravagant lascivious loving of the curve,
There, right there between the bottom of the
  buttocks and the thigh,
Where skin meets skin at true right angles
  with an arithmetic symmetry,
weighty and delicious,
  and there the eye resides.
  Even if the angle be obtuse or acute,
Either way I plunge into the hungry distances beyond,
  along the curve within that fragrant ether,
    like all of space and time is happening at once,
  the coming and the going,
Like I'm there and not there like a particle
  within a hidden probability,
Where I'm caught without a net within the
  mesmerizing trance
Of the ever-present underpants.

It is forbidden, but it is as much myself as anything.
My noble lofty works or my lonely subtle jerks,
My sweetly earnest lovemakings, my bungling awkward
  leave-takings, they are parts of me.
There is nothing other than the one, the all,
  the whole and lovely creature that I am.

I love the gentle curve of binding energy between
The taut point of the chin where the head is taught to
  join the neck, then continue on its way
Down to nether regions, the sweetly subtle
Body of desire where all things are as yet to come,
Through landscapes all esophagus
  of eating and dissolving, ingesting
Then revolving in a sutle rhythm to the core,
Where tutelage begins of the pleasures I am wanting
  but as yet are unfulfilled,
                    not yet solving, which keep
  hanging like a dangling participle, like a
  chord not quite resolving

And the endless mystery of how my longing can be
  so vaporous yet can feel so solid,
  the riddle of my need, of what I want
and what I wind up getting
    somehow mingling into one
  and the delight of then forgetting
   in the heady joy of giving,
everything is coming and
                  becoming in a bewildering fulfillment.

I am you and you are me and
We are all together, it's been said.
    Sex is what we call it but we might as well say love,
  for there is no other land within the body
wherein the sex can dwell.
The two both come together, inextricably are bound,
  and wound around each other like the number sixty-nine.

I find you in a dream, hidden cryptic in the text,
  or rolling in the hay amidst the sex,
   in a body not my own that is molding to my will,
  as mine is melded into you and in the dream we do yes
continue this comingling and conjoining.

It is the dimple right above the cheeks,
    indented there into the skin under the sheets,
       right above that sweetly round behind
           of the one I seek that
                turns me on the most of all.
             I will linger there,
Wherein I am myself as much as anywhere.

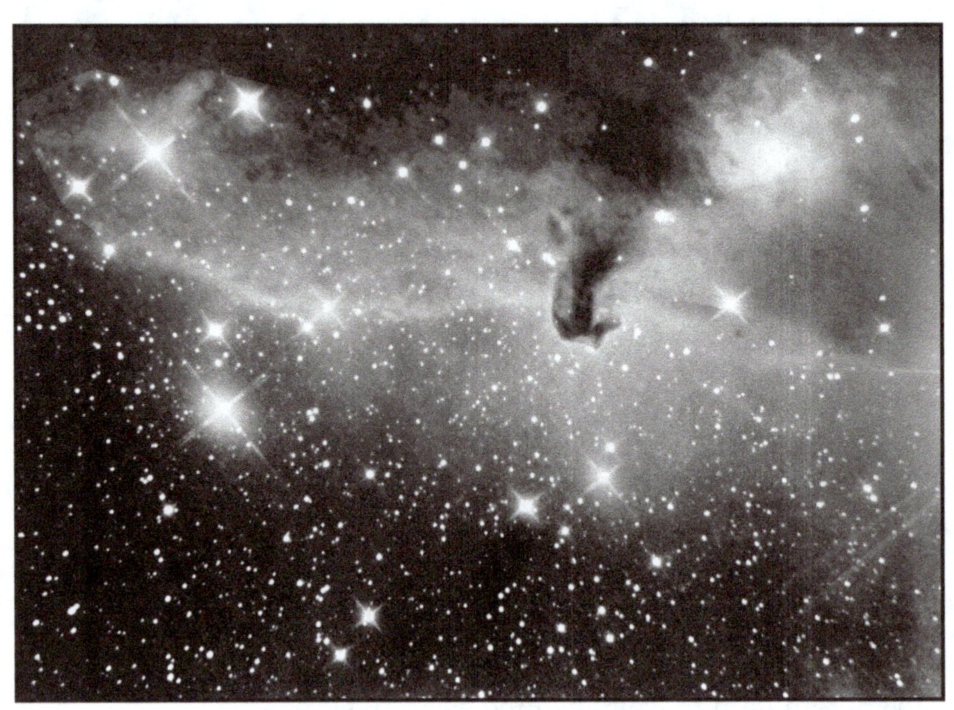

Where Folds Intersect

I will write with words and without:
  a poem unspoken.
I will see what is visible and not:
  a spirit through skin.
I will find what is present and absent:
  where folds intersect.
I will form the black disc of the moon
  along the curved inner edge of my eye
Betrothed to the wedding ring of sun,
  dwelling for a moment both without
And within.

No one can say this is wrong,
  for none of us can know these things.
Nor can one speak of right, for stars and
  stones know neither virtue nor sin.
None can pierce that veil of nebula
  in which stars and moons gather
Together in longing, then drift in
  their separate orbits apart,
Nor can one unfold the mystery
  of another from the hidden realms
Of the heart.

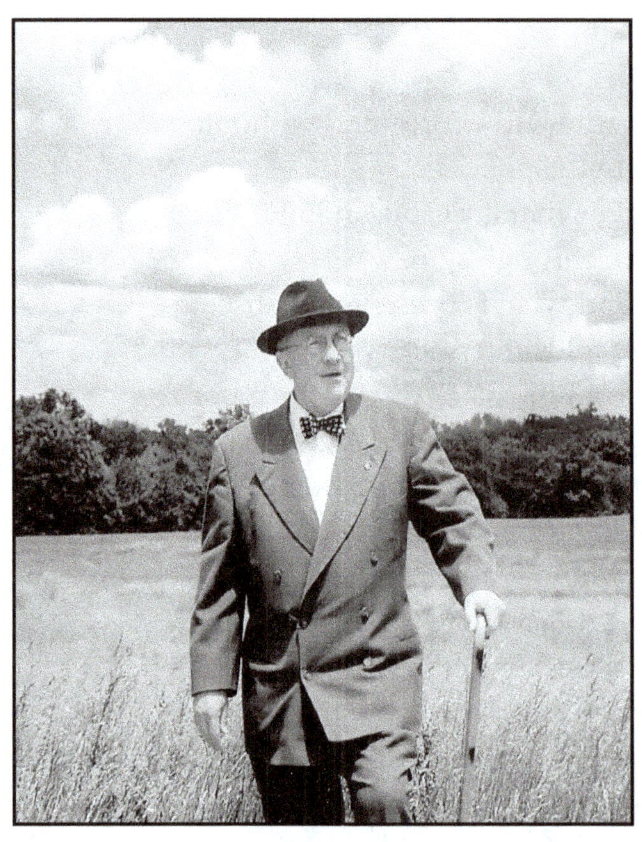

Raymond Starzmann
1945–2019

Portraying President Harry Truman near
the Truman Farm Home in 2014

Presidential Scholar | Historian | Reenactor
| Scholar | Speaker | Master Librarian to the
Nelson-Atkins Museum of Art | Friend to
All He Met

Grace

A trick of physics: everyone he met was his best friend, whom he would treat as long-lost brother.

As well you felt that you were his, even though you knew he had so many others.

And the stories! They would hold you rapt, captured in his spell of timeless true adventure, even as you wondered how he recalled them all!

He saw your gifts and had his own rare gift of gentle nurture, so that, unaware, you moved at his suggestion toward who you would become, and with this special magic he could thus affect the future.

Democratic down to bone, he practiced every day those lessons that he spoke, a true and honest man in these best of times, worst of times, that so precious time he dwelt among us.

Planting seeds of tolerance and brotherhood was his special art, which he voted to a place in us from which they will not soon depart.

When he ascended, heaven needed little help to lift him, for he had formed his life into a flower light as air.

Thus when his noble grace rose tall enough to kiss the sky, it was but the softest breeze that was needed to carry him aloft, to ferry up and over this so loving, this kindest, this dearest of the gentle men.

Leaves

Wet leaves on the path
Surprise themselves with their new
Colorful wardrobes

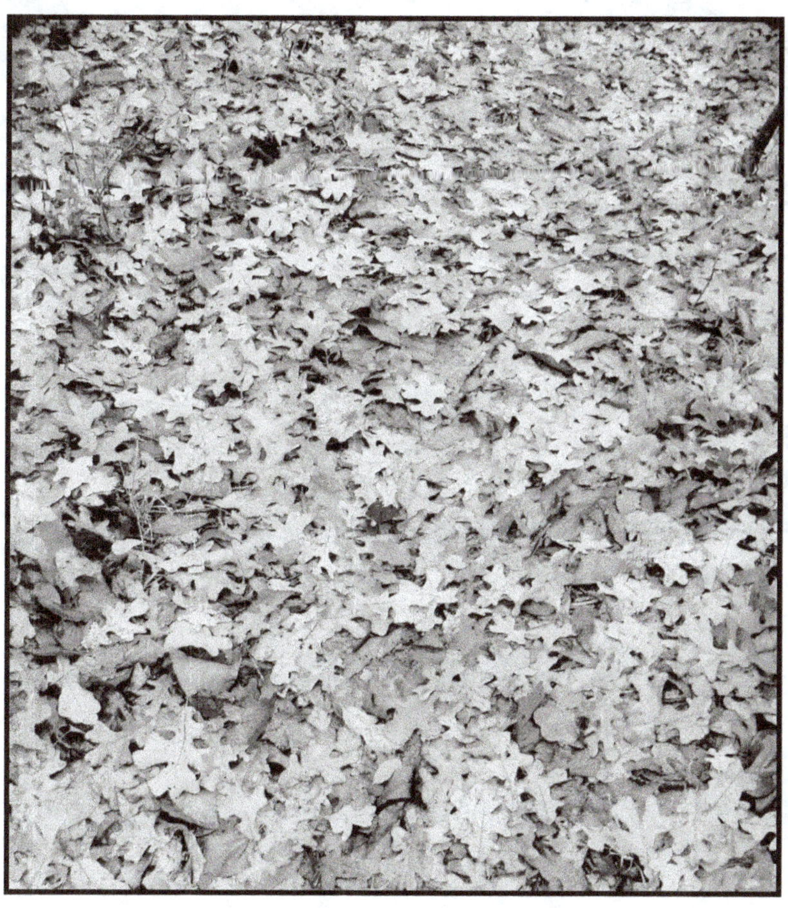

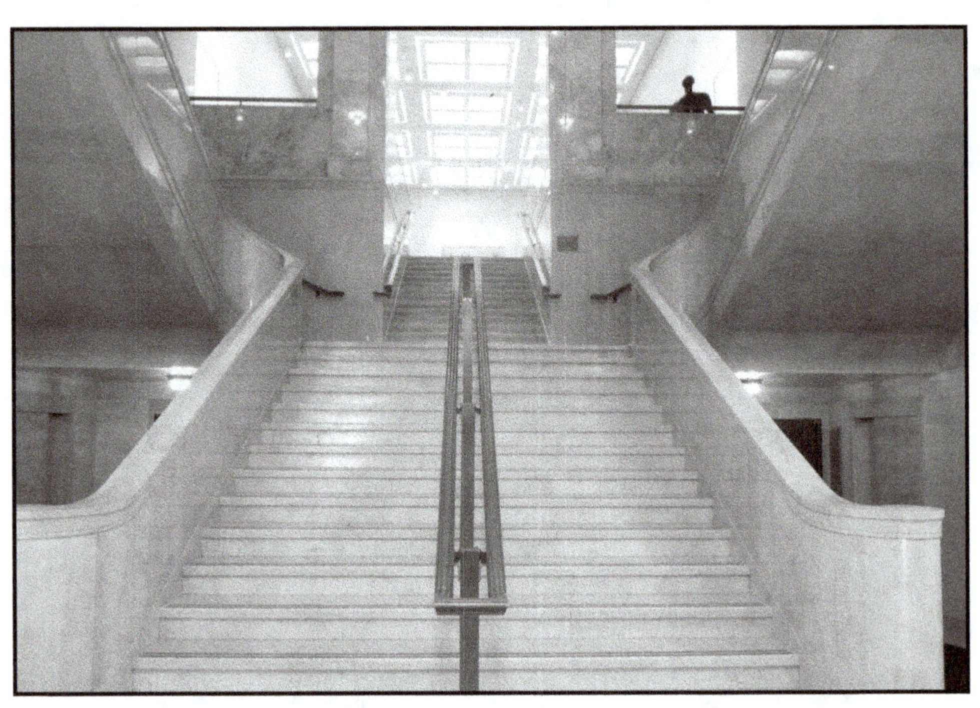

The Museum Stairs

We two flowing out over waves of prairie,
  wild as the flowers we fly across, reaching out
  for one another, pink petals opened.
Laughing, you toss teasing questions to me,
    then your eyes, like emeralds, their touch
  so like a wind I could follow.
  I run to catch up, and up, ecstasy like Theseus' thread
Unraveling loose in the giddy air.

I remembered this half a lifetime later as
you chased me through all the rooms of the museum,
    Up the wide marble staircase into the antiquities.
We laughed together, then toyed with
  a few sweetly gentle iniquities.
  You held on to me as playfully as you would a feather
  that had found the path of your hand.
I flew in close to cherish
  the joyful sweetness of your body
  like a zephyr wind that even then I sensed
I would never be light enough to sail upon.

I could wish an arrow into being, so to pierce us now
  as then, when we were such
small and tender children
  among the wildflowers, so simple.

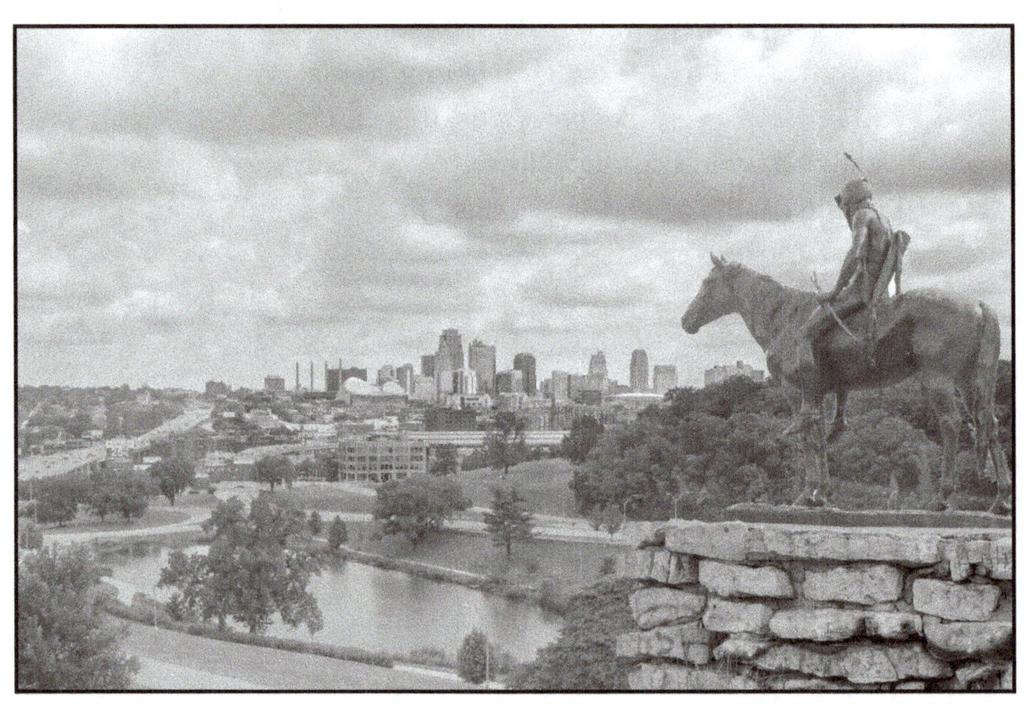

Kansas City, Here I Come!

Come to Kansas City, it's a crazy little town!
North's a little crazy up, Southland's crazy down.
East side you can walk about as fer as you can go
West will take you out of state. Not out of KayCee, though!
It's a great big city, yes, but crazy as it sounds
It's small enough to know the name of everyone around.

We folks are crazy happy about lots of things we do
Drinking beer from Boulevard, eating crazy barbecue,
Crazy for our Negro Leagues ~ that's baseball, by the way ~
And just about any sport that we can watch or play.
Oh, lots of other crazy stuff that Kansas City has
Like our world-famous boppin' hoppin' crazy jazz!

Want to dance, hear music, buy some art or see a play?
Right here on the prairie you can do it every day.
Some other towns claim fame in these particulars, it's true.
But none with quite our plain old crazy mix of old and new.
We're compared to other places like Chicago, New Orleans
But we can boast the best of both and tucked right in between!

We've got culture, local art, performances, and books
Lots of places to enjoy them, too, in cozy little nooks
Or in great big concert halls or venues small and varied
To watch or listen, dance or sing and have the spirit carried.
From the Kemper's crazy art, Nelson-Atkins' painter's bliss
To spoken word, crazy stories, or dope poetry like this!

You talk about our atmosphere? Man, we got some skies!
You can see the far horizon as a storm begins to rise.
Clouds ten miles high full of lightning and a-spittin'
Hail or rain or sleet or snow with which we'll soon be smitten!
But if you don't enjoy the weather here out on the range
Just hang around five minutes more and likely it'll change.

You needn't travel far to visit nature, birds, and bees
In summer you can hardly see the houses for the trees.
And parks and fountains, my, oh my, to get your outdoor fix.
You'll never have to go too far before you're in the sticks.
And the city's simply gorgeous here at any time of year
Every season has its beautiful and special way to cheer.

You think we don't have problems? No city is without.
Disparities of race and class and culture? Yes, no doubt.
But we have secret weapons of which not all towns can boast:
People who are caring and who love to give the most.
We work to right injustice, fill a stranger's empty cup.
We'll not rest until we know that all are lifted up.

We're makers and we're builders, we love to get things done.
With can-do spirit, solving things is what we do for fun!
Building bridges over differences until they realign
To heal the Troost divide, or the one along State Line.
We join the friend and stranger into one community
We delight in helping others, whoever they may be.

We'll roll up our sleeves. We'll work hard until it's done.
Our neighbors taken care of—have we forgotten anyone?
Wrongs are righted, slights forgiven, love extended, ever.
All accepted. No exceptions! We're all in this together.
We're healers and we're helpers, we cannot let things rest
Until all wounds are mended, until all persons blessed.

Though I am not a native, my love for it has grown
So much so that now I call this crazy town my own.
Among the many reasons it has captured my attention
(Including all the ones that I have previously mentioned)
Is one that's best of all, I think, when all is said and done:
They got some crazy little women here. That's how I got me one!

Geese

Geese in the western
Sky sing their joy in movement
Wedded to sky, free

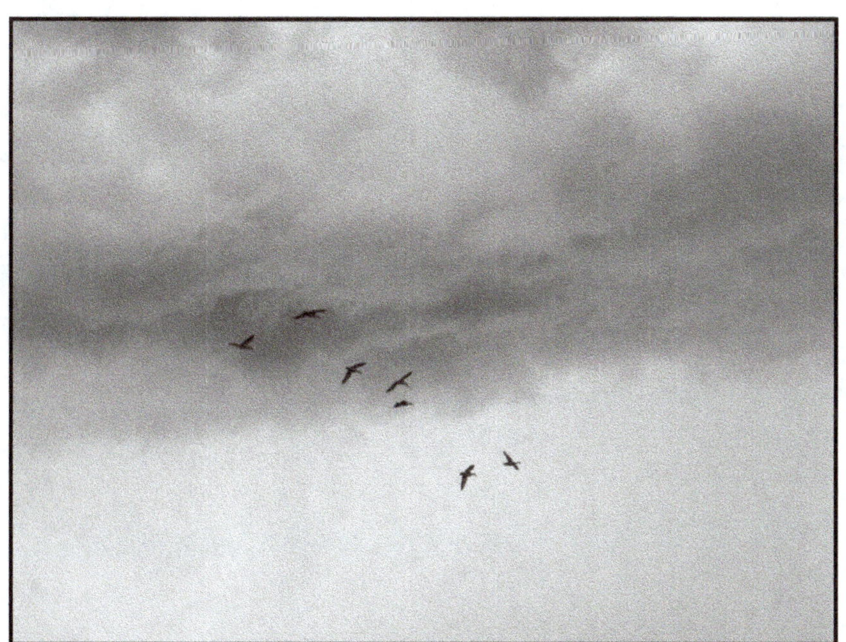

Three

Mirror

A Mountain

Simple mountains are
The most difficult ones to
Climb without falling

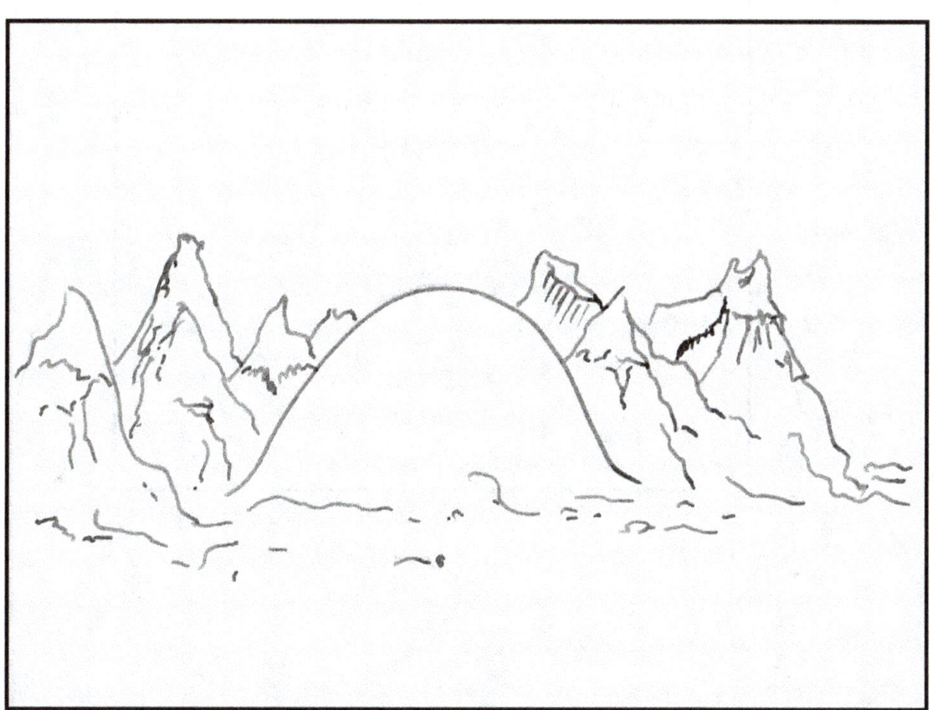

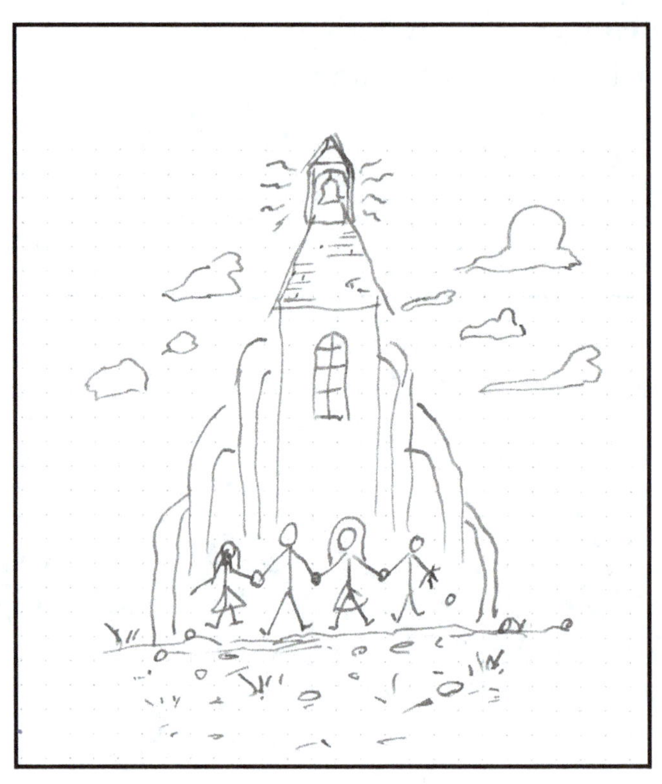

Churches of My Fathers

I bolt in claustrophobia
   from the churches
   of my fathers

Run out to the world to
   find a god larger than
   stale wine and wafers

Long-dead ecstasy and
   revelations forgotten like the
   genesis of ancient statues.

No matter the rituals they
   kept, no matter the paths
   of others faithfully followed

I never quite knew them catch
   fire to burn with their
   own flames of passion.

I want to shout Look!
   Your truth has left the
   building! Find him in the

Nearest daisy in the lifting of
    tides in the movement of stars.
    Rituals cannot contain him.

Sunday morning but also blue
    Monday, bad days and good,
    morning by morning he grows.

Or maybe this disloyal speculation,
    this running with scissors, wrongs
    them. If there is table in heaven

And god is so vast, there will be
    seating enough somewhere for all
    who are here and who hunger.

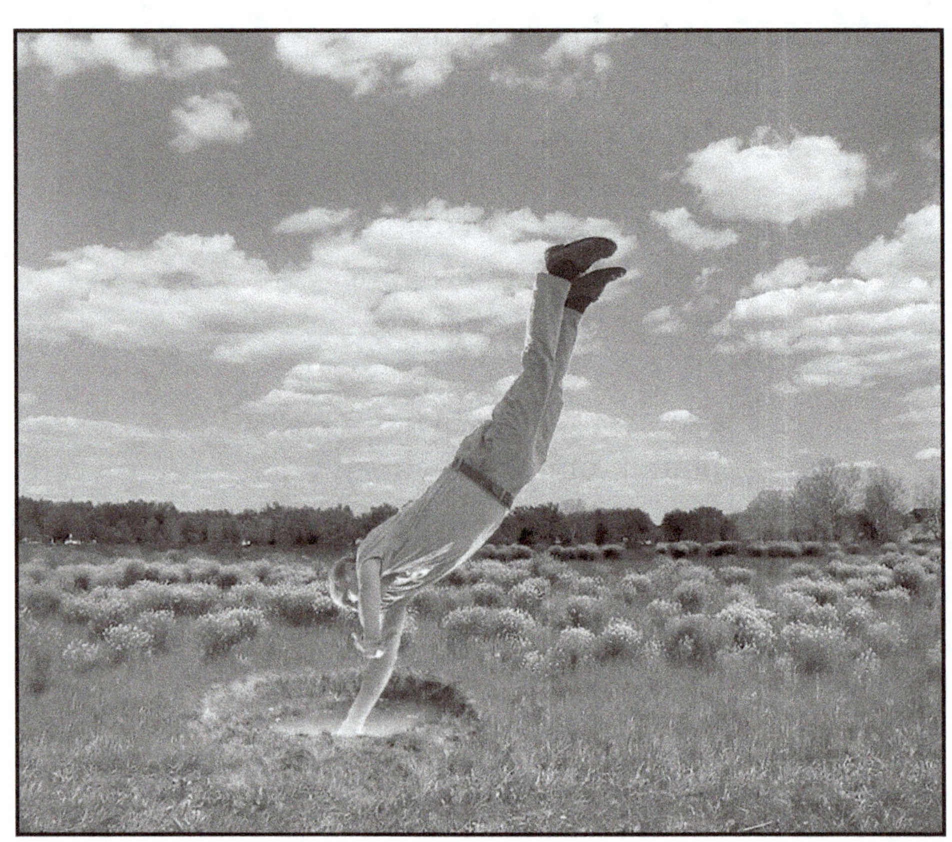

Falling Into Holes

Walking through the garden,
I happened on a hole. Distracted, I fell in.
I didn't reappear for quite a while.

It was not a good hole, as it happened.
How could I have known? Novice in the
hole-falling skills as I was.

Now, some rabbit holes are a wonder,
  because they lead you to a place
  mysterious, enchanting.
You learn and grow and heal yourself,
  like a hero on adventure or a
  searcher after antiquities.
For if you knew everything all at once,
  how good would that be?
So if you fall down these holes
  or jump in, just wait for the fun to begin.

I walked on by another hole. Here, I
used my sense of smell (ten thousand times,
I've heard, less acute than that of any hound, but still)
to tell if this was Wonderland or other. I sniffed
  and sniffed until my nose began to itch.
This time I recognized a trap.
If I fell in, the tasks and worries would begin
to consume me from the outside and besiege me
  from within. And I was ripe for taking,
so unless I learned from my mistake
  I would keep right on a-making.
That was my sense.
  I moved on.

My life
   is a falling in and out of holes.
I come upon them in the glade
   or mist or in the darkened shade of forest,
not so secret as most folks might suppose.
These precious holes are rare but when you find
   one, you know it. Go on, take the leap!
The different parts of you will grow together
   like the bark of an old tree, which can work itself
around open wounds to enclose them in
   precious gnarled burl.

I soon learned to tell the good holes from the bad,
      and if I felt a sense of dread, I let them die into my past.
            But if I sensed adventure, maybe mystery,
some baffling deep confounding history, or a Zen koan or
puzzle to be solved before I could begin, I would fling
   myself within and so would start the healing
of the gaping hole in me.
   I would recognize a kindred down in the world of the mole.
Alice might happen by to give me pointers, speak of Rabbit,
   talk to me of bad Queen and the wonders of a Hookah.
And Eeyore, his blessedly self-deprecating self,
   would be there, and Roo and Tigger bounding,
   and the perfect, very perfect Pooh and Piglet.
I am their foundling in the Hundred Acre Wood.
They are there waiting for me Oh!
   to grow up then fall down.

Crow

I am crow, clever
And wise. I can see around
Corners and through lies.

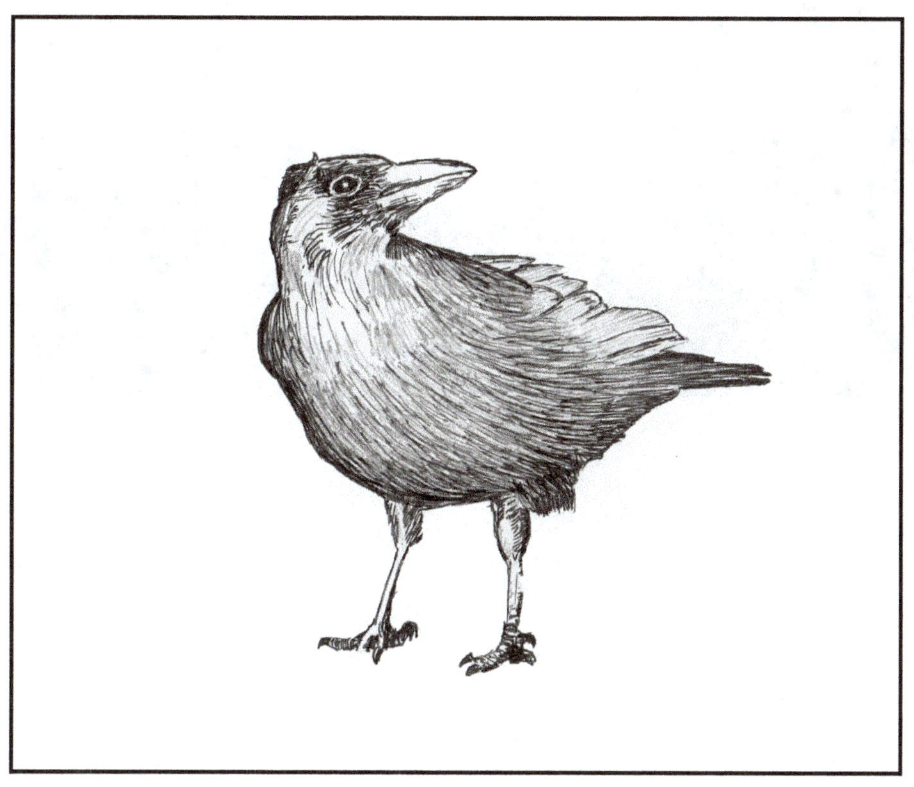

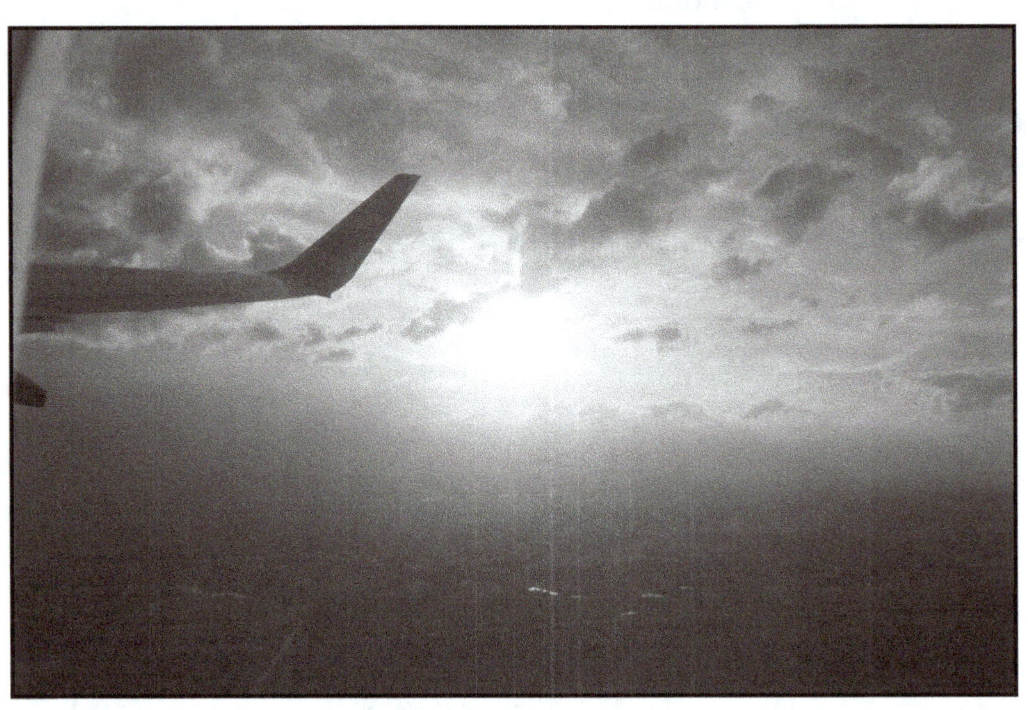

I'm Flying, I'm Crying, I'm Dying

How to survive Houston to LA? All I have is a clipboard and pen,
forgot my water, can't find my Zen.

This will just have to do until then, I'll curl up here in a ball and write
myself into a poem.

Van Morrison blows through my ear, something off the Veedon Fleece
album. "It's the woman in you, it's the woman in you," he sings to me
over and over.

Noise cancellation headphones are junk. It's the woman in me who's
so sensitive. Can't hear myself think. Can't feel my body, can't tell my
sex or whether it's blue or it's pink.

TV's in rhythm on the backs of the seats
Over our faces their bloody deceits
Here we are lined up in long rows like pews,
Receiving the gospel: the sports and the news,

The movies, the action in multiple waves.
My writing will save me! My writing's what saves.
Barely room for my knees, clipboard is
skewed at like forty degrees.
But soon I can see that I've filled up the page,
I kind of go crazy and flip it in rage,
It falls to the floor, into the aisle, the stage
where only the crew can perform.

We hide in our seats, my poetry sprouting like Yeats.

I glance down the aisle for the flying instructions
But they come on the tube as a Disney production!
Some random flight crew is playing themselves,
Are they stoned or psychotic? They're dancing like elves.
They're trying real hard, they're going through motions
But nothing's real cute about ditching in oceans.

It's the woman in me.

Van the Man. The woman in Van.
No peace, this is madness, I'm writing sideways,
the music goes through me. Madness!

I'm cramped but alive, all others asleep at thirty-two thousand,
feet in the aisle, the sprawl is contagious,
the pen just fibrillates, filling up pages.
Finally, enough! I push the call button.
Four minutes, five minutes, six minutes, seven.

There she is! What's the problem?
"How do I turn the TV off?" I shout over the roar.
She's stunned as if nobody's asked her before.
She points to a button the size of a dime,
there on the armrest the whole goddamn time.
Push it, she says, again and again.
A volume icon drops down from ten.
The TV goes off when it finally hits zero.
She walks away smugly. Must think she's a hero.

Me and the woman in me go back to the writing.
The TV pops on again, pimping, "I'm just so EXCITING!"
It was my elbow! If you push the button,
which you can't help but do,
the insidious thing takes over for you!

Devices on laps like prayer books in church.
We're strapped in our seats as the plane starts to lurch.
The air is in waves but we're flying straight through.
Is that Oklahoma where the wind's whipping through?

Writing like madness, the plane is now curving now swerving now
swooping now tilt up your tray table praying the woman with manly
voice saying.

The woman in me sits upon seat, feeling, for that is what women do
best, and because shaking and turbulence and what rhymes with ur-
bulence? Madness, I say, this is madness!

Van Gory, Van Morri, Van Gogh, Van the man Morrison,
Van Dyke like a woman slides through my head,
earworm that lets me know I'm not dead.

We're cutting through air in a big silver bullet, or knife.
The blood of my wound is making me swoon for my life.
Because somewhere over the South, or the North Carolina,
The woman in me felt someone pierce her vagina.

I look out the window to find out our status
A thin hazy fog or a thick cirrostratus
Either way we are lost and alone.

I don't want to be here! I want to go home!

Outside the window the world goes black
There's no moving forward, there's no going back.
Are we over or under the planet of Venus?
I'm holding on hard, hard on to my penis.

The man in the moon with a silver spoon and the man in the woman
in me. All I can see is the pen flying over the page and the woman in
me and her rage.

I hear someone say "Please take your seat or I'll beat you to an inch of
the door and what's more I'm the beast with the maker's madness!"
Or maybe I'm now reading minds.

Van Gogh and Van Morrison, Toni and Morrissey, all the things I can
take out to sea. Madness!

The only things left to hold on to my sanity:
Pen and a paper, Sean and the Hannity,
Stewardess row in the back like a cannery
Sitting with Steinbeck and Keats and old Flannery.

They are no longer patient but past it,
Have reached the end of their rope and at last, it's
The end of our wonderful Customer Service!
They're wondering if and why they deserve us.

I'm writing them up. I'm turning them in.
I'm writing them off!
                    No, I'm writing them in.

Cause we're all of us trying while flying through space
To find enough room to fit in.

I'm writing it down, I'm writing it out.
I'm writing it on what I am writing about,
  and all of this writing is touching upon
The subject of me and the object of you,
The woman in me that I'm writing through,
The grammar of what a life sentence can do
Here in a box that irretrievably locks
Each one apart from another
And from the one thing that could save us:
Awareness.

A deep kind of knowing that what we've been sowing
And under the radar just keeps on growing
Is a gut-wrenching, soul-rending, heartlessly unending
Bestial bitch of a
Madness!

Enlightenment

In the wood, sudden
Happiness kisses my face
Dances outside words!

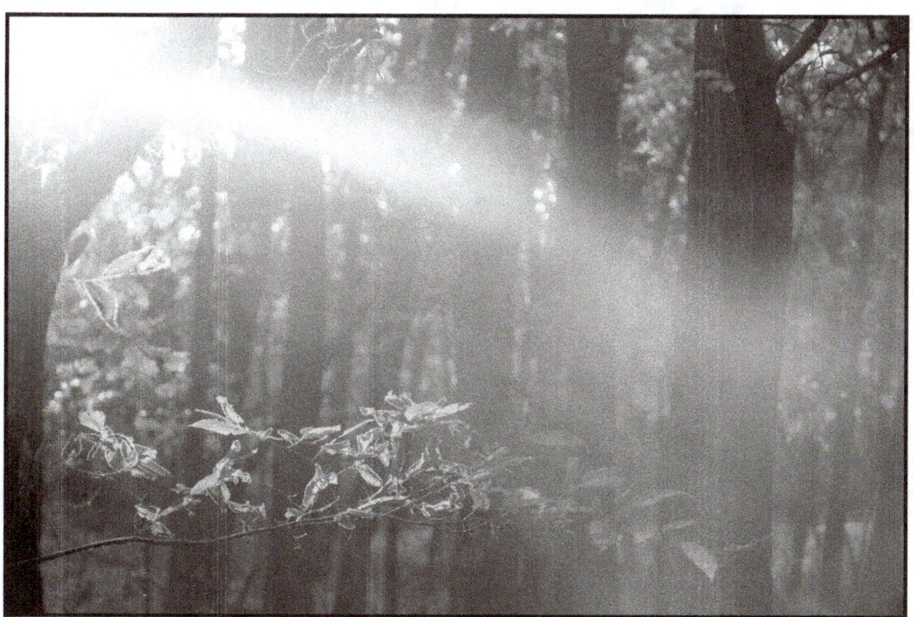

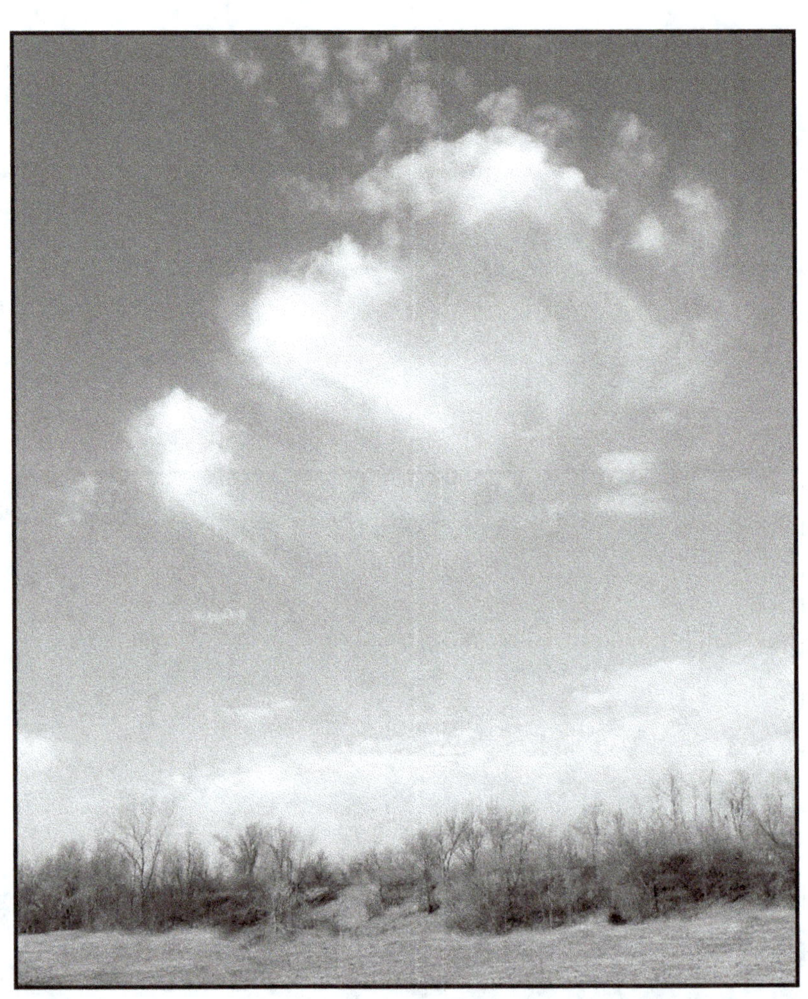

Poetry in Air

There is a bridge to happiness
  within the heart somewhere
Whose path is paved with poetry
  in the middle of the air
When we begin the writing of
  our grief, despair, and pain
Stepping-stones of words lead out
  then back to heart again

With fear in every pore we boldly
  take the pen in hand
Painful detonations serve
  to show us where we stand
Small grenades of truth begin
  exploding from the tip
The web of our illusion and
  denial starts to rip

The words will hold our weight aloft
  but only if we dare
Speak them bold and clear enough
  to hear them everywhere
To resolve their shape and sound
  and wrap our voice around them
Find their hidden meanings and give
  thanks that we have found them

Though they've always been there,
    ever present, ever near
Only when we're still enough
    do we begin to hear
They are a compass in the world
    whose navigation's true
Pointing toward a wisdom
    that we already knew

There is an angel on the side
    of poets, so they say
But she is there for anyone
    who speaks to her this day
Listen to her, breathe her in,
    find words that are your own
And with your words for company
    Begin the journey home.

Full Moon

Alien invasion!
Golden orb of mother ship
Hovers in the east!

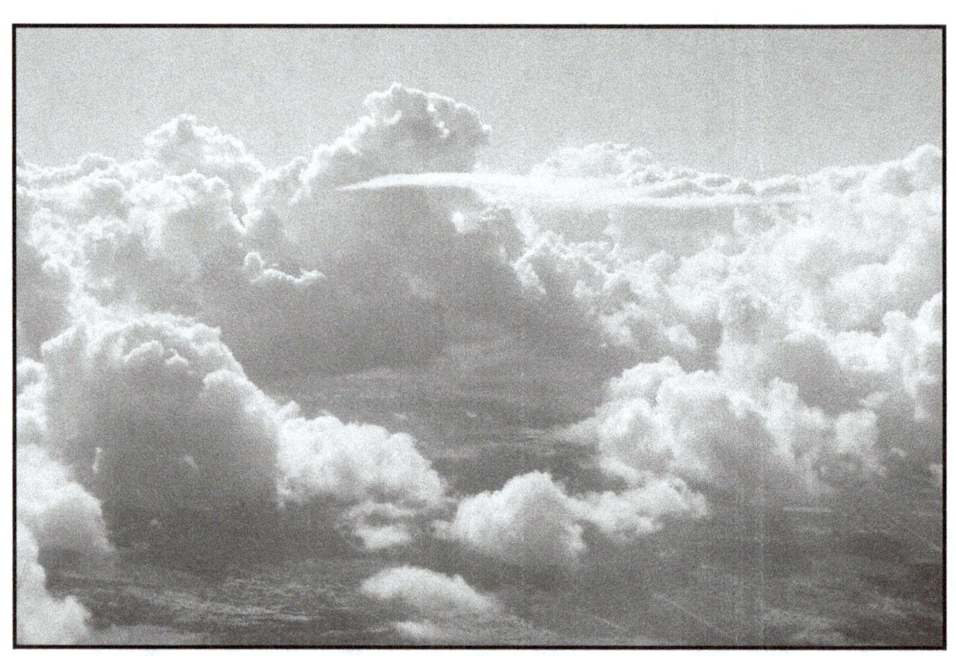

My Heaven

Let this be my heaven now
In place of pillowy cloudtop elsewhere, elsewhen,
Let this my single blade of grass suffice.

Show me how to know my hurt and joy as sacred.
Open me in love with others. And my heart,
Open it to roses red,
And blood and rainbows after rain
And so purifying pain.

Let me ready body so that
When my joy appears, I can live it open
and can share it with my world.
Let this world and my body in it
Be my heaven now.

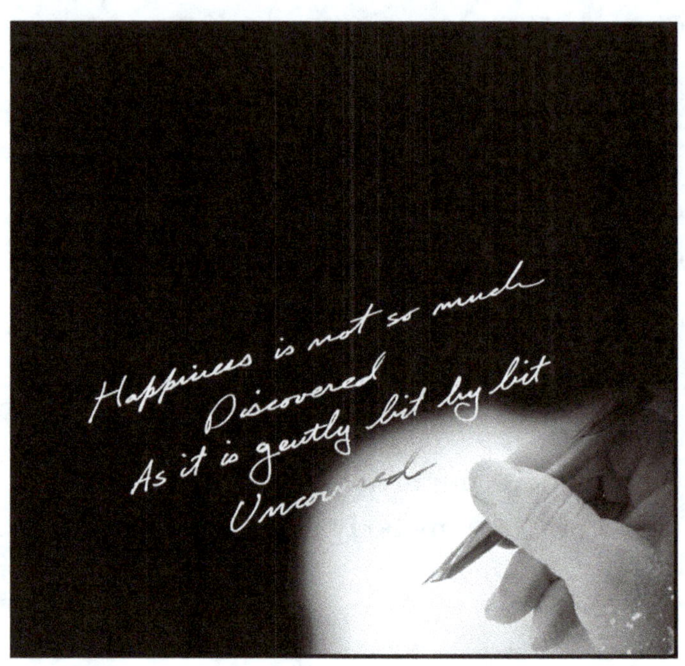Happiness is not so much
Discovered
As it is gently bit by bit
Uncovered

Pen To the Hilt

Pen like sword goes in to the hilt,
This pen full of ink that can write what I think,
This weapon so razor-sharp it cuts to the bone,
But only if honed and only if wielded where
I am not shielded from sharps,
Those surgical blades that cut so I bleed
But the wound of the truth is just what I need.

The pen uncovers the baldest of lies,
Especially those that I try to deny.
When the writing is done and then I revise,
Whatever remains is the truth.

The biggest lies are those from my youth,
Gifted by family I needed to heed to survive.
They only knew what they knew
But Father didn't always know best,
And he held his cards real close to the chest.
Mother's whole life was a kind of a test.
When she died, it was marked incomplete,
So she passed on the passing or failing to us.
We babes were burdened with her albatross.
An impossible task: making up for her loss.
How could we help but fail?

The pen says write. Keep writing and writing, it says.
Write that it's time to stop blaming others,
Friends or lovers or fathers or mothers,
For though at first it might be instructive,
After a time it is counterproductive.
The blaming of others is self-destructive,
For they did unto us what was done unto them,
They merely gave what they got.
This is the way dysfunction keeps right on repeating
Down through all the begats and the new generations,

Unconscious repeating of depredations
In iterations that look so different
Yet always exactly the same.

Once we grow up then we get to choose
To live as we did or we can refuse.
Shunning the mantle bestowed by the past
We can end the cycle at last.
The only path out of the pain
Is to reshape the inherited self,
A personal catch and release where we can first
Tag ourselves with a band round the wrist
So we can always be found.
Then we can run the risk of discovery,
Begin the task of recovery, bringing to life
The joy that we missed.

The pen in our fist at the end of our wrist
Allows us to hear our own voice.
We write it down for the record,
Then roll up the paper and stuff it in bottle
And fling it out wide on the sea of ourselves.
When later we stand on the shores of our bounding main,
We pick up what looks like the finest champagne
We pop off the cork and we read the message
So simple and true: "I love you, I love you, I love you."

With pen in hand you can shatter the mold.
You can write yourself a new freedom to cherish and hold.
You can grow a new skin and then wriggle out of the old.
You can take a new name and shed the clothing of shame.
You can start living where life is forgiving,
The pain of the past is no longer reliving
And everything's new and everything's waiting for you.

So take pen in hand and be bold.

New Moon

Imagination—
Or is there really a gold
Thumbnail rising up?

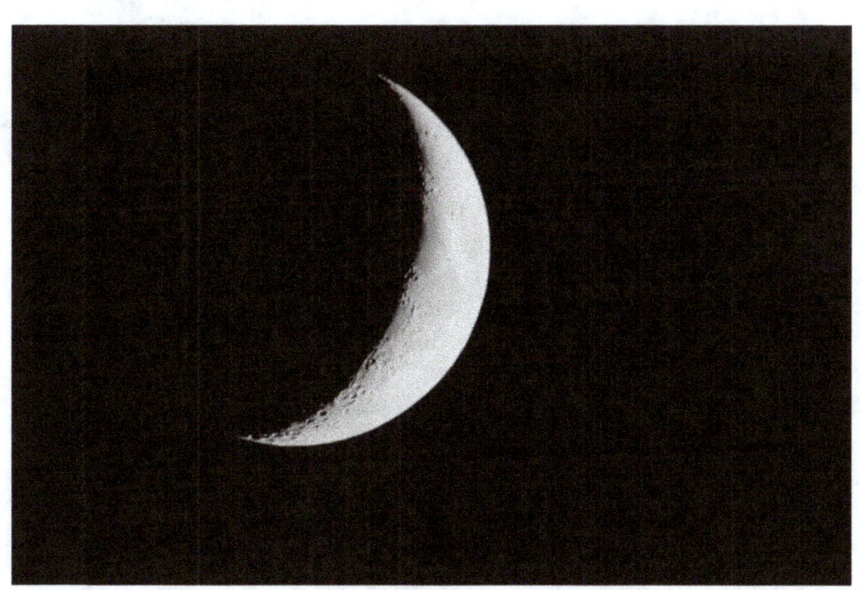

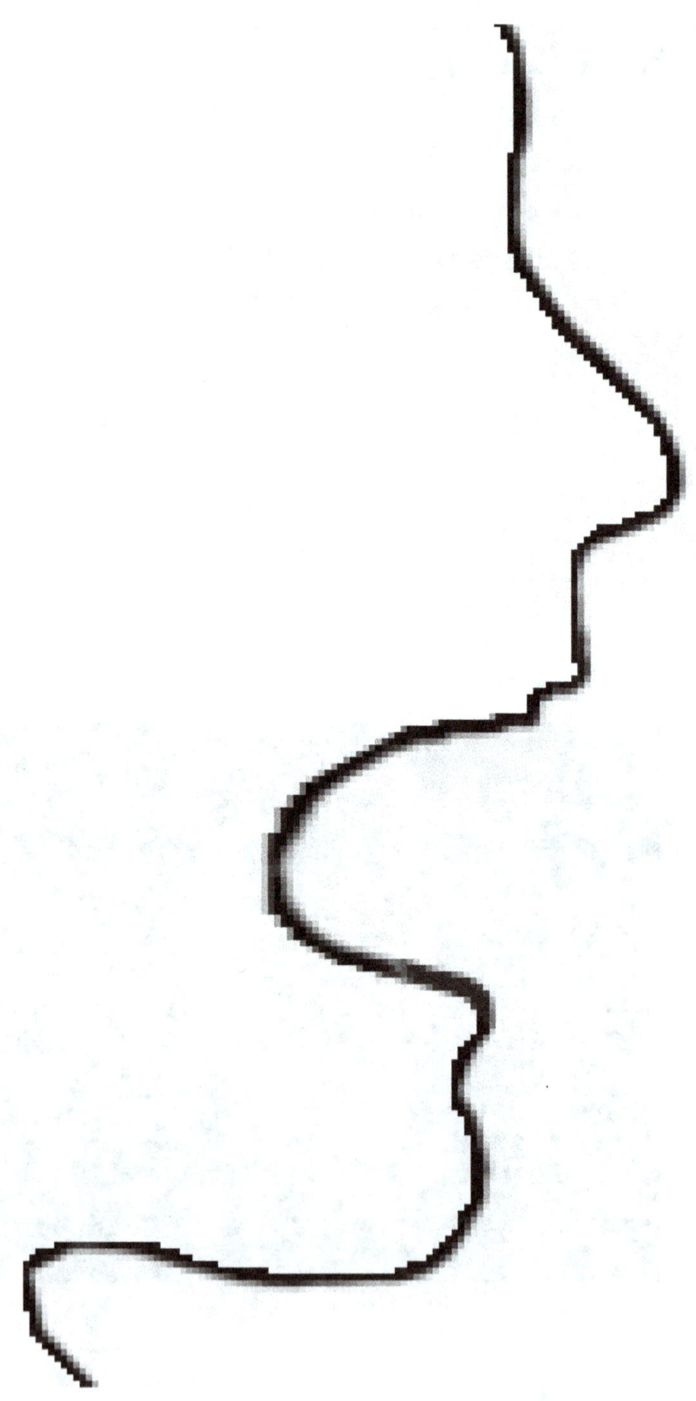

Pukey at the Slam

What is this Poetry Slam thing you guys got going on? |
That is so oxymoronic! Not even oxy, just moronic! |
Poetry is all flowers and twittering birds |
and angels in heaven and stuff |
and Slam is like mud wrestling except |
without the ban on steroids and brass knuckles. |
It doesn't make sense. Why don't you have |
an Underwater Feather Toss? Or Olympic Curling with |
Live Beehives? Or Styrofoam and Tissue Paper BattleBots? |
Who cares? What's the point? What does it mean to win? |
And why do I want to so badly? |
Okay, then, I'm in. I'm gonna take you on. Watch this. |
I'm going to melt the wax on poetic. |
Look up Poem in the dictionary and it'll say, "See David." |
Clear out the women and children |
and put on your masks, because when I get really exercised |
I use up all the oxygen in the room. |
Dope himself will hear this poem and go, "That was so dope!" |
I'm gonna hang out here dangling on the end of a long thin rope. |
In three minutes you'll need to wash out your ears with soap. |
And I'm gonna win in the end because that's what I do. |
I hope. |
Here goes. You ready? |
Damn, this is scary. Not as easy as it looks. Stop shaking, David. |
Is this mine? I don't remember writing this. |
Don't ask me what this means, it's deep, okay? |
If you can't figure it out |
that ain't my issue, Kerouac. |

Look, Grasshopper, once you get here yourself |
you're gonna realize form is the only function. |
Okay, watch real close, I'm gonna be moving real quick here, |
soon as I get my mouth working right. |
Here we go, this is the beginning. Ready? |
Okay, here's the middle. |
Hold on to your hats, ladies and gents. |
This is where it gets real dicey. |
It'll look like I'm reading a rhyme |
or maybe it's some kind of meter, |
doesn't really matter cause it's only live theatre. |
Maybe I'll show you the depth of my heart |
or maybe my pain and my anguish |
at the embarrassing size of my peter, |
or how that reminds me of Pepper Eater, |
and how that rhymes so well with Derek Jeeter, |
whoever he was. |
I'm gonna roar and jump on the stage! |
I'm gonna rage and stomp on the floor! |
I'm gonna do it again and again |
and pretend like I am giving you more! |
Shouting bad words in a kind of a rave |
that'll make George Carlin curl up in his grave. |
And then the piece of resistance, you ready? |
I'm gonna shout out my generic, all-purpose, |
generalized, non-specific outrage! |
I'm gonna spill real blood up here |
just by reading off of the page. |
That's the reason you came here, right? |
Just keep your eye on the stage. |
Here it comes. Wow. There it is. |

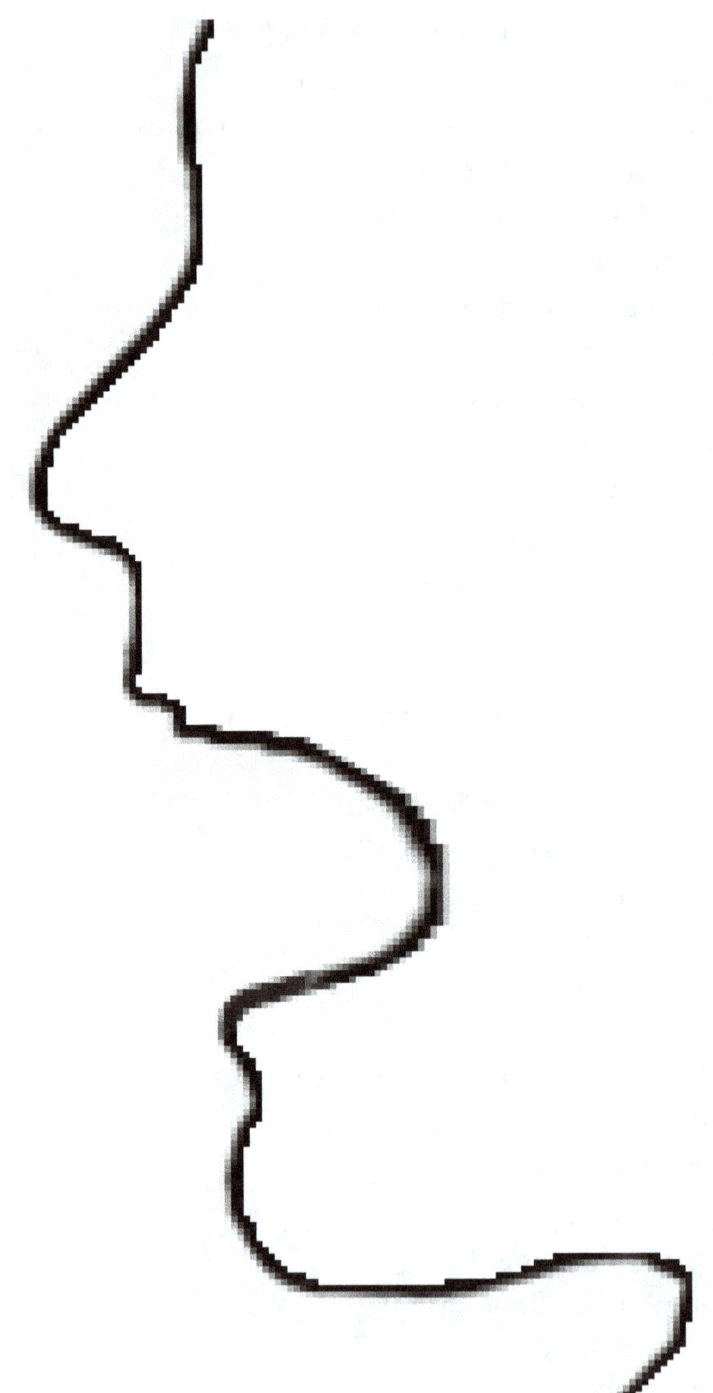

I think there's some right there in the middle! |
Or maybe in a riddle it's a little bit of spittle, |
or maybe it's a puddle of vomit, |
the sputtering tail of David's Comet |
as it comes spewing out of the void. |
But it felt real heavy so it must be blood |
Cause I could hear it land with a great big thud. |
Either way it's okay, relax, I think I'm done.
I'm finished, I'm spent, it's over, I hope I won. |
Put up your scores. Don't make 'em all tens |
or the swooning of winning'll give me the bends. |
Just show me the money and glory, |
that's kind of the end of the story. |
But hurry it up, I need to move fast, I gotta run. |
Because here at the end of the day |
when the fat lady finally sings |
and all is literally said and done |
and you move on to other things, |
you'll have a chance to review the tape |
and you'll realize it was only ketchup.

Performed at the monthly Poetry Slam hosted by
the Poetic Underground in Kansas City, Missouri,
at their location at The Brick, June 6, 2019.
I didn't win.
It was a rousing success!

Mountains

Simple mountains are
The only ones that can be
Scaled without climbing

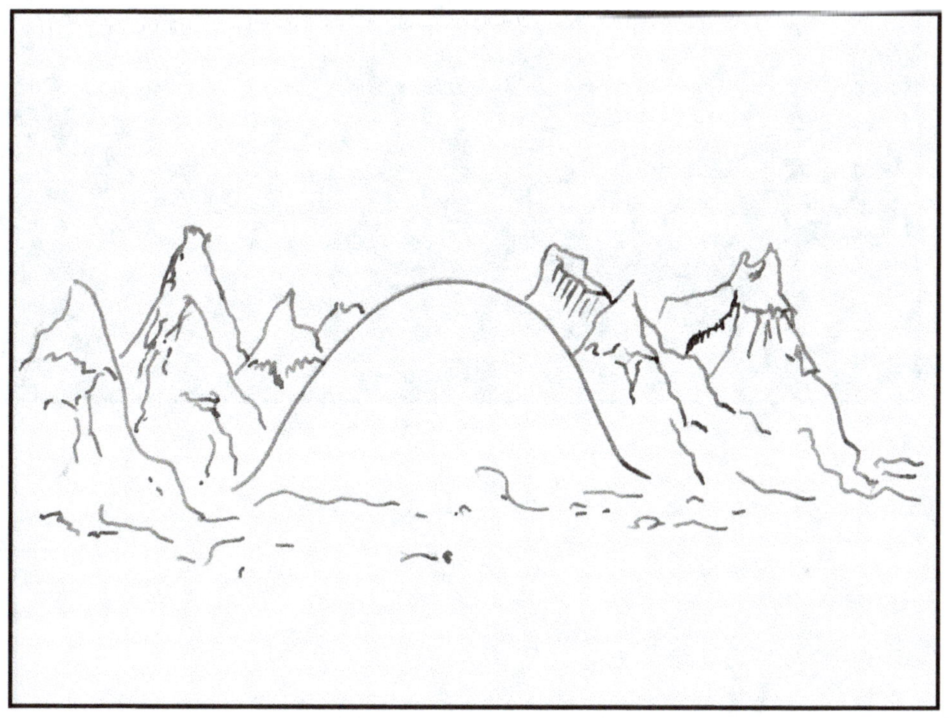

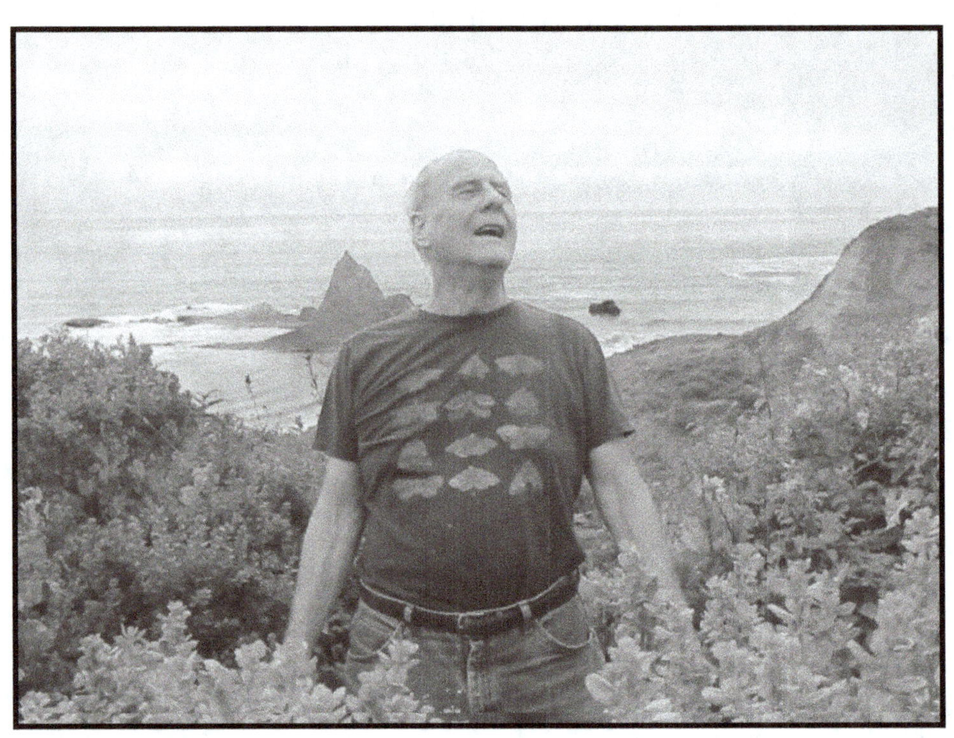

Sea Shanty

I'm gonna go to sea and I'm gonna find out what I'm made of
I'm gonna find a place where I can finally hang my shoes
I'm gonna fill my sails with adventures full o' wonder
What they'll be is a mystery so how can I refuse?

I'm gonna live life lusty
I'm gonna live life bold
Not gonna let my ship get rusty
Never gonna let my heart grow old

I'm gonna sail the seven seas till I find myself a new one
One nobody's ever seen before, so I'm gonna be the first
I'm gonna dive down to the bottom, talk with the brand-new fishies
I'm gonna drink the water so I'll never die of thirst

Oh, I'm gonna go out larkin'
I'm gonna go out drunk!
On the joy of life and barkin'
At the moon until I lose my funk

I'm gonna go a-soaring on that great big wild blue yonder
I'm gonna get as high as I can get and touch the sun
I'm gonna find out what it's all about or I'm gonna die tryin'
I'm gonna find out what it feels like when I've finally won.

I'm gonna laugh my laughter
I'm gonna cry real tears
I'm gonna live my own life after
Living everybody else's all these years

I'm gonna set my ship exploring great big world around me
I'm gonna cut 'er loose and let 'er sail off like a kite
It's the way I heal my sorrow, just like when I was a baby
I'm gonna find my innocence and I'm gonna shine my light

I'm gonna go out larkin'
I'm gonna go out drunk
On the joy of life and barkin'
At the moon until my ship gets sunk!

Oh, I'm gonna live life lusty
I'm gonna live life bold
Not gonna let my ship get rusty
I'm never gonna let,
   never gonna let,
   never gonna let my heart grow old!

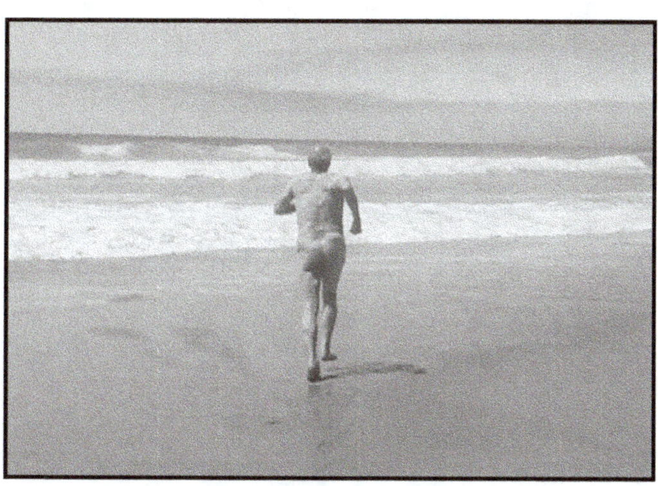

Sea Shanty

Transcription by Amory Bottorff

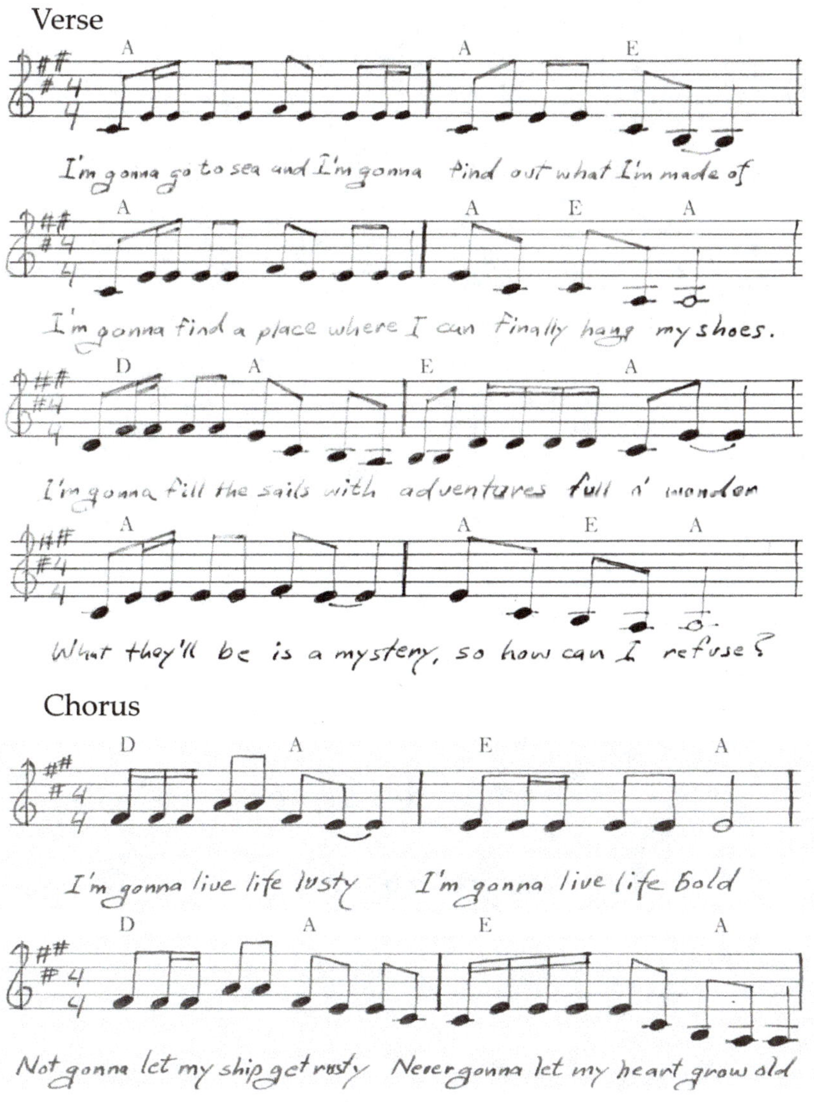

Video of Sea Shanty performance and more at
https://www.youtube.com/user/skyboyphotos

For Mary Oliver

1935–2019

Old Poets

Old poets never die
They float off astonished by
The taste of the sky

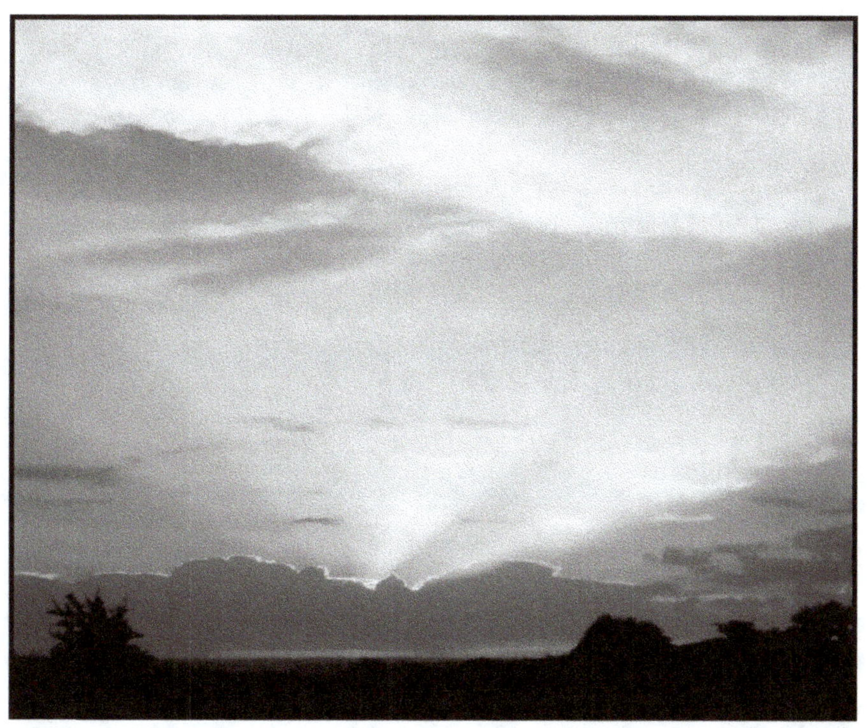

David Robert Thomas Bayard

is a furniture maker, photographer, and writer who carries a deep love of nature and a fascination with the mysteries and contradictions of the human spirit. His writing draws upon his experiences as an Army lieutenant, rock band performer, circus roustabout, homesteader, and artist.

He lives on wooded acreage in Kansas City, Missouri along with his wife, Pamela Whiting, writer and journalist. They have a dog and two cats, all three of whom recite poetry in their native tongues.

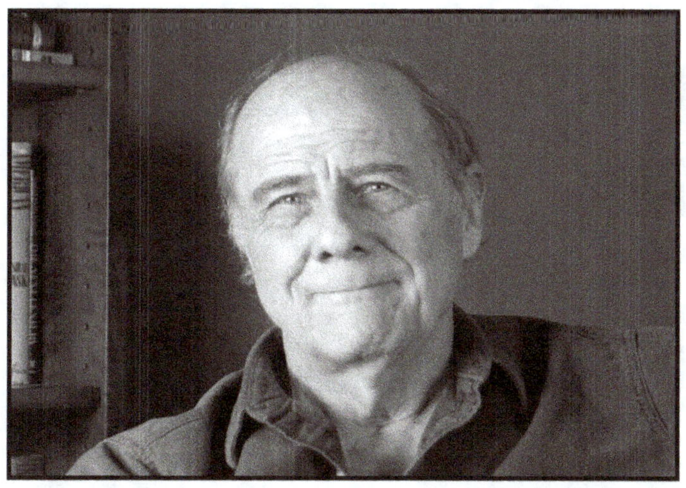

David can be contacted by phone at 816-765-0080 or
by email at db@skyboyphotos.com

Find his books, prints, cards, and calendars at

www.syboyhotos.com